Chameleon Days

Chameleon Days

An American Boyhood in Ethiopia

TIM BASCOM

A Mariner Original
HOUGHTON MIFFLIN COMPANY
Boston / New York / 2006

For information about permission to reproduce selections
from this book, write to Permissions, Houghton Mifflin Company,
215 Park Avenue South, New York, New York 10003.

Visit our Web site: www.houghtonmifflinbooks.com.

Library of Congress Cataloging-in-Publication Data
Bascom, Tim, date.
Chameleon days : an American boyhood in Ethiopia / Tim Bascom.
p.   cm.
Includes bibliographical references and index.
ISBN-13: 978-0-618-65869-5 (alk. paper)
ISBN-10: 0-618-65869-6 (alk. paper)
1. Bascom, Tim, date — Childhood and youth. 2. Ethiopia —
History — Revolution, 1974 — Personal narratives, American.
3. Ethiopia — Description and travel. 4. Americans — Ethiopia —
Biography. 5. Missionaries — Ethiopia. I. Title.
DT387.95.B365 A3   2006
963'.06092 — dc22   2005031530

Book design by Melissa Lotfy

PRINTED IN THE UNITED STATES OF AMERICA

MP 10 9 8 7 6 5 4 3 2 1

The following chapters were previously published: "Baboons on a Cliff," in
Boulevard; "And I'll Fly Away," *Florida Review,* winner of the 2004 Florida
Review Editor's Prize in Nonfiction; "A Vocabulary for My Senses," *Missouri
Review,* winner of the 2003 Missouri Review Editor's Prize in Essay, also
published in *Best American Travel Writing 2005.*

The following songs are quoted with permission: "Surely Goodness and Mercy"
by John W. Peterson / Alfred B. Smith. Copyright © 1958 Singspiration Music
(ASCAP) (Administered by Brentwood-Benson Music Publishing, Inc.).
All rights reserved. Used by permission. "His Sheep Am I" by Orien Johnson. Copyright © 1956 Orien Johnson, assigned to Sacred Songs (Division
of Word, Inc.). All rights reserved. Used by permission.

All photos taken by Kay or Charles Bascom and reprinted with permission.

*This book is dedicated to the many
missionary children, known and unknown,
who carry their own stories inside them.*

*In particular, it is dedicated to
my brothers, John and Nat, and to my
lifelong friend Daniel Coleman.*

Contents

Foreword

AFRICA, the site of our primeval origins, possesses as a conse-
quence enormous reverberations for many Westerners and North-
erners. The beauty, magnetism, risk, and potentiality beckon am-
biguously, however, because alongside the kaleidoscope of noble
skyscapes and splendid fauna bespattering the veldt can lie a parallel reality of famine and pandemics, or horrific politics. And if the
imagery becomes phantasmagoric, this isn't China, but our Africa!

In *Chameleon Days*, Tim Bascom recalls being airlifted at the
age of three from his early childhood in Saint Joseph, Missouri, to
Soddo, Ethiopia, by vaguely dogmatic missionary parents. That
alchemy—a child's-eye view of arduous immediacy—is main-
tained quite admirably in his memoir, forty years later, thus
breaching the standard traditions of travel writing. Although his
father was a doctor, not merely an evangelist, his medical responsi-
bilities theoretically encompassed a hundred thousand patients.
So the row they hoed was not easy, and the family did burn out
during a second tour of duty, leaving prematurely, although both
the author and his parents returned in later life.

But it's an Africa of basics, not numinous romance: a tale well-
grounded in a little boy's close-grained focus on apprehensive innocence and vulnerability. There's heat and cruelty, kindness and
leprosy, revolution and elephantiasis. Yet since a lot of Tim's ex-

periences are located in the missionary boarding school in Addis Ababa where he was often marooned, for him it may be even more conflicted and scary, with the kinks and quirks of Orwell's *Such, Such Were the Joys* added on.

There is logic and mercy in Africa too, and these peep through during the Bascoms' hapless, jolting Land Rover excursions, and in new friendships, along with the contradictions between what missionaries want to accomplish yet need to shut their eyes to. Charity must keep office hours, or a nervous breakdown could wipe the family out. Tim climbs into a cedar tree for a personal refuge at Bingham Academy, and into the foliage of a huge avocado tree in Soddo (while eating avocado sandwiches his mother makes for him) to escape what seems untenable. He even spies upon the Lion of Judah, Emperor Haile Selassie himself, from its leaves.

Not a book of war and pestilence, this is about childhood, much of which, for almost any of us, is going to be composed of "chameleon days." Tim, however, has a chameleon, plus a loving family to cushion his continental displacement, and now writes with meticulously graceful recapitulation about pet pigeons, or the weaverbirds and snakebirds at Lake Bishoftu — turquoise in its volcanic crater — where they all vacationed.

Africa's somersaulting mysteries and difficulties compound this schoolboy's natural anxiety at juggling self-respect with popularity, and how to remain a Christian when served by servants, then seeing his omnipotent father rendered puzzlingly powerless by infighting. Place and populace meld here in a lovely narrative, styled for transparency. A childhood's jitters stand recollected in tranquility — and a beloved continent, ruefully enigma-riddled, in maturity.

—EDWARD HOAGLAND

PART ONE

Baboons on a Cliff

AS WE LEFT the Addis Ababa airport and started across the city, my brother Johnathan and I stared out the windows of the Volkswagen van like dazed astronauts. He was six and I was only three, but we were both old enough to sense that life might never be the same. A torrent of brown-skinned aliens streamed by on both sides, treating the road like a giant sidewalk, their white shawls and bright head wraps bobbing as they weaved around each other. Donkeys and oxen bumped into the van, whipped along by barefoot men in ballooning shorts.

After sixteen hours in an airplane, we found that our whole world had disappeared. Gone was the quiet stucco house in Saint Joseph, Missouri, where we had lived while Dad began his medical practice at the state hospital. Gone were the tire-thrumming brick streets of Hiawatha, Kansas, where we were given candies and back-scratches from Grandmother. Gone were the maple trees and the old-fashioned street lamps, lit up like glowing ice cream cones. We had stepped onto a Pan Am jet in one world and stepped off in another, as if transported clear across the galaxy.

Our driver braked for a truck being unloaded, and children pressed their faces against the glass, shouting, "*Ferengi, ferengi,* hey you, my friend, give me money." They left mucous streaks on the windows and patches of breath that faded as we drove on.

Older, broken people approached too, holding out open palms.

DEBRE BIRHAN, ETHIOPIA, 1964.
The new missionary family. Me in front.

"*Gaetoch, gaetoch,*" they murmured, using the Amharic term for *lord.* A legless man on a wooden scooter shoved himself into the road and thumped on the sliding door with his tar-stained hand. Next, a fingerless woman thrust her stump through the open window by my father, and my brother Nat, who was not even six months old, began to whimper.

"It's OK," Mom whispered, even though Nat was too young to understand. "She just wants money."

"What's wrong with her face?" I asked, having a three-year-old's curiosity about the woman's caved-in nose.

"It's leprosy," Dad said. He gave the woman a coin. Then, as the van eased away, he called back to my older brother, "Johnathan, do you remember any lepers in the Bible?"

Johnathan was quick with his answer: "Yes. The ten that Jesus healed!"

I wanted to be just as smart. "I know that story," I yelled. But no one seemed to notice.

• • •

Subject to their parents, children learn to adjust. When our parents moved to Ethiopia in 1964 to become missionaries with the Sudan Interior Mission, my brothers and I spent our first two days and nights adjusting to an environment from which we would soon be thrust, forced to adjust again. Blissfully unaware, Johnathan and I ran footraces around the hallways of the three-story tarpapered guesthouse. First, we raced down our second-floor hall, dashing toward a color print of Jesus the Good Shepherd. We turned sharply in front of this Jesus, who was leaning out over a cliff edge to hook a lost lamb with his crook. Then we sprinted onto the open balcony, where we could see to the lawn through thick wooden railings. Elbowing each other on the stairs, almost falling, we stumbled onto the grass and galloped back along the asphalt driveway, past the clinging purple-and-white fuchsia and up the stairs that led right to where we had begun, the hall where Jesus hung with his shepherd's crook outstretched.

At night we bedded down with our baby brother in a room that had uneven adobe walls and shiny blue enamel paint. A dividing sheet could be pulled across the middle like a shower curtain to cloister us from Mom and Dad and their candle. However, we still couldn't sleep — too disoriented by jet lag and car lights on the ceiling, too pumped up by all the change. We picked at cracks in the wall, exposing hardened mud and flecks of straw. We whispered to each other and flipped our pillows to put the cool side on top. And when we woke at noon — barely in time for lunch — we lay paralyzed on our metal-frame beds, sweaty under the wool blankets and not sure if we were in the right story. Everything felt so jarring and out of place: the unexpected belch of diesel trucks below our open window, the haze of exhaust fumes floating into the room, and the weird babble of foreign voices drifting to us on the crisp, high-altitude breeze.

Soon came our second major adjustment. Mom and Dad were told to report to language school four hours north of Addis in the Amhara highlands, which meant Johnathan had to start boarding school immediately. An elderly missionary drove us to Bingham Academy, the school set aside for all the children of the Sudan Interior Mission, and we simply left Johnathan there, standing next to his new dorm mother, a squat woman in a gray wool skirt.

Johnathan's face crumpled as we drove away, one eye squinting against the bright tropical sun, one hand lifted in a weak salute. He looked smaller than he should have, standing in the middle of the red cinder parking lot.

Mom cried. She cried all the way out of Addis Ababa even though she tried to hide it, biting her lower lip and looking out the window of the van. Dad reached over and rubbed her neck as the vehicle climbed, switching back and forth up a thin mountain road. We passed hobbling donkeys half-buried under stacks of wood and hay. We passed stone-walled houses with thatched roofs, roosters that scattered at our approach, and little top-knotted boys who wore only shirts and waved so high that their privates showed.

Every time that we got close to the edge of the road — where the sky took over and I looked down on nothing — I fought back a wave of vertigo.

"When will Johnathan come to see us?" I asked.

"Soon, Timmy. Soon," Mom replied, wiping the corners of her eyes and turning on one of those terrible smiles that signaled unspoken sacrifice.

But a week after we had settled into our little two-room apartment at the language school in Debre Birhan, high on the plateau above Addis, Johnathan still hadn't come and I still didn't have anyone to play with. Mom and Dad were busy studying Amharic all day, and Nat was interested in nothing but Mom's breasts or things small enough to fit into his mouth. As for me, I was left in the care of an Ethiopian nanny whom I refused to acknowledge.

Another week passed and Dad received a message sent by radio from the academy. He looked grim. I could hear him whispering to Mom in bed after the generator had been turned off and only a candle guttered in the next room, sending yellow light flickering up the walls.

"I'll go down with the supply van," Dad murmured. "If he sees me, he won't feel so far away."

"He's too young," Mom whispered back.

"Maybe, but what else can we do? They all go to the academy."

"Not the Stuart children."

There was a pause before Dad spoke again. "You know the rumors. Everyone says they'll end up misfits."

My mother sighed. It was one of those deep sighs that she allowed herself only when she was away from the other missionaries.

"He's too young . . ."

"I know," Dad whispered back. "I know . . ."

The next day, when my father went down to Addis Ababa in a supply van, I hoped maybe he would come back with Johnathan. He had sounded as if he might. When he returned alone, I quit thinking about my older brother. Letters still came each week, always starting with the same blocky printed words. Mom showed them to me, mouthing the words slowly — "I am fine. How are you?" — but that didn't sound like Johnathan really, and it didn't give me anyone to play with.

Finally, my brother *did* arrive for a brief, weeklong break, brought up the escarpment in a Volkswagen van along with several other boarding-school kids, a crate of Lyles Golden Syrup, and five boxes of Amharic New Testaments. We all hugged him, even Nat, who was getting old enough to imitate us. At my turn, Johnathan smiled shyly, embarrassed. His arms stayed at his side. He wouldn't listen to anything I said, glancing away toward Mom and Dad as if they might vanish. Only after I had snatched the dark blue Kansas City Athletics cap from his suitcase and run away did he pay attention to me.

"That's mine," Johnathan yelled, and he lunged, accidentally knocking my head against the stone fireplace.

"Johnathan!" Mom scolded him. "Remember your age."

Suddenly, too quickly, he was all apology, patting me on the head and placing the cap there. "You can wear it," he said. "That's OK."

But it wasn't OK. I had taken the cap because I wanted him to forget Mom and Dad and act normal. Instead, here he was patting me like a newborn puppy and looking up at Mom as though desperate to please her. This was not the Johnathan I remembered from before we left him at boarding school — the boy who had chased me down the guesthouse hall and past Jesus the Good Shepherd.

Johnathan stayed unaccountably meek until, with only two days left in this short holiday, Mom and Dad planned one last family activity. They gathered several other missionary families and took us hiking. While Nat rode on Dad's shoulders, Johnathan ran with me on the rock-strewn slopes. Unencumbered by fences, the two of us raced wild. At last I had my brother back — the carefree one who wasn't thinking too hard to simply be.

Johnathan chased me over the crest of a little hill. Then we both stopped dead. We were completely unprepared for what lay before us: an immense drop-off that stretched away a mile to each side, as if marking the edge of the world. We had both been so engaged in our immediate surroundings, celebrating the hummocky green ground and the rocks under foot, that we were stunned by this abrupt end to the landscape.

Mom and Dad caught up with us and drew in their breath. The other adults came up too. They all exclaimed as if watching a particularly good display of fireworks.

Then someone spotted something we had overlooked — a herd of baboons huddled in the grassy hollow to our right.

"I can't see them," I complained.

"Look down my arm," Dad said. "Now can you see them?"

I nodded, sobered by how close the animals really were. The big males had lifted their gray beards and were grimacing with yellow fangs. The silent females stared suspiciously, while wide-eyed babies climbed the fur on their bellies.

Malcolm, an English missionary with bright blond curls, whispered, "Now for the show."

"Malcolm," his wife cautioned, but too late. Already he had

begun galloping down the slope directly at the herd of baboons, yelping and caterwauling.

Pandemonium. The panicked baboons split off in two directions and stampeded. One cluster came right at us, then veered to the cliff. The other cluster wheeled around Malcolm and raced half-circle to rejoin their comrades. And all the terrified babies sent up a chattering wail as they clung to their mothers.

When I saw the baboons bounding toward me, I scrambled up my father's legs, clutching frantically at the sturdy cotton of his shirt. They bolted by on both sides, running pell-mell toward the cliff. At the edge they didn't slow. Without pause, they leapt into space, leaving behind just the grass and the wind and the African kite gliding high above, wings still as welded steel. Then I screamed.

"It's OK, Timmy," Dad insisted. "They're gone now. Look, you can see them climbing down."

Malcolm came loping back up the hill, his face red with exertion. He echoed Dad: "Really, lad, take a look."

Even Johnathan jumped in, acting as if he were another adult: "It's not that big a deal. See. I'm not afraid." He grabbed at my bowed head, trying to force it off Dad's shoulder; but I only protested more shrilly. Dad had to carry me right to the edge of the cliff and turn around, waiting until I had the nerve to open my eyes. Then I did see the baboons. The whole clan had reassembled and was rippling down the sheer rock-face like a muscular brown liquid, descending so quickly they seemed to be falling. The infants, still clinging to their mothers' bellies, bobbled and stared up toward me. They made no sound as their primal families dropped away, sucked into the abyss.

"Don't be such a baby," Johnathan said, which hurt because it came close to the truth. I still felt terrified in a panicky, helpless way. The rapidity of the baboons' descent tugged at me — made me feel I must go too. I gripped Dad more tightly and wouldn't let go even after he stepped back from the cliff edge. As our group reassembled and started across the rocky plain toward the language school, I stayed perched on his shoulders, refusing to get down despite Johnathan's offer to race me to the next tree or rock. I wasn't in such a hurry now to outrun my brother.

Eventually, Dad began to sing in his rich baritone voice: "Surely goodness and mercy shall follow me all the days, all the days of my life." Then Mother joined in, her cheeks flushed red from the cool breeze and the exercise and the happiness of the wild open spaces. Her clear soprano rang out like a hand bell, and the rest of the group picked up on it. They became one big walking choir belting out the lyrics: "And I shall dwell in the house of the Lord forever. And I shall feast at the table spread for me."

Little Nat had fallen asleep in a sling that Mom had rigged on her back from a native shawl, a white strip of cloth called a *shamma*. Safe on Dad's shoulders, finally I joined with the other singers, compelled by the unified sound of our group. I imagined our voices carrying for miles, lifted on the cool wind and blown across the treeless pastures: "Surely goodness and mercy shall follow me, all the days, all the days of my life." Could the wind carry those words all the way to the edge of the great escarpment above Addis Ababa? Could it carry the song down the mountainsides to the distant city, even to the walled academy where Johnathan would be returning to school?

I looked to my older brother walking alongside Mom, his hand almost touching hers as it swung back and forth. His lips moved with the words of the song, but I couldn't hear his voice. Eyes fixed on the horizon, he seemed to have already gone.

The Chameleon Looked Both Ways

I WAS OFTEN ALONE after Johnathan's visit ended and he was taken back down the long, steep escarpment to boarding school. My parents went back to work. Each morning they met with the other missionaries for three hours of intensive language practice, leaving Nat and me with the brown-skinned nanny whom I still refused to acknowledge. She smelled of wood smoke; that was all I knew.

I clung to Mom's skirt as she and Dad walked out of the apartment. I dragged along behind them, clear to the steps of the classroom, with the nanny close behind balancing Nat on her hip. They had to pry me loose at the door. If I tried to squeeze in, the Ethiopian language teacher blocked my entry, closing the door as if I did not exist. I stared at the hard, varnished wood, wishing I could walk through it unseen.

As I waited, the dew steamed off the lawn of the language school. Nothing else happened. Bored, I clambered over the porch railing, so that I could stand in a bed of poinsettias and peek through an open window. I ignored the clucking of the unwanted babysitter. My parents were inside, and I wanted to be closer to them.

Today, I could see Dad with a spike of short black hair on his forehead. His blind eye drifted — the eye whose sight he had lost at age sixteen in a freak accident at the firing range. Where did that eye look, I wondered. And what did he see there?

I watched Mom too, with her electric way of smiling, her cheerful red cheeks and white teeth. I concentrated on her especially. I knew that she was more likely to look back because mothers generally looked at little boys more often than fathers did.

Occasionally, she gave me a furtive glance, hoping that I wasn't focused on her, but if her eyes met mine, she smiled wistfully and turned back to the language teacher.

"*Ta-nayis-tilling,*" said the teacher. "That is how you may say 'Hello.' Then you can ask '*Dehenah na chew?*', which is to say 'How are you?'"

I climbed back onto the steps, sat down, and listened, still refusing to look at the Ethiopian nanny as she cuddled Nat and called to me from the lawn, using her own strange version of my name — *Timotheus*. I could pick out Mom's high, clear voice echoing the teacher. I sat and listened and tried to say some of the words myself, joining the whole chorus of voices that parroted these strange words back to the teacher.

"*Ferengi,*" he announced.

"*FERENGI!*" they replied, and I mouthed the word too. I had heard this word often because children shouted it whenever they saw me. They chased us white people with this word, grinning as if we were clowns or street performers.

"This word is for *foreigner*. You know it, I'm sure. But really it is not from Ethiopia. The Italians brought it during the World War Number Two, and so our people learned to call all foreigners by one word. I am afraid you will be hearing *ferengi* all the time while you are in Ethiopia. Please repeat it. *Ferengi.*"

I stared at the poinsettia plants next to the steps, with their incredibly green leaves and brilliant scarlet flowers.

"*Ferengi,*" I said.

That's when I saw the chameleon. Three inches long, it blended in — jade green — with the leaves of the poinsettia plant. Holding its body still, it spun its bulbous eyes, each one gazing a different direction, scanning the two hemispheres for danger. Only after five minutes did it take a cautious step.

Teetering, twitching, it took another step.

I held back, wondering if I could be poisoned by a creature so ugly, but after a while I screwed up the courage to poke the leaf it perched on. At this disturbance, the chameleon clenched into a rigid, crouched stance, as if surrounded by predators.

Neither of us blinked. Neither moved. We played a silent staring game, lulled into contemplation by the fat bumblebees that droned over the snapdragons and by the rhythmic call-and-response of the language class. The chameleon had one eye fixed on me, but the other swirled, looking for something else to anchor it.

"*Gi-delem,*" said the instructor.

"*Gi-delem!*" replied the class.

"This is a very useful word in Ethiopia when things do not work as you please. It is the same as 'It does not matter.' Please let me hear you again."

"*Gi-delem!*" I said, leaning toward the chameleon.

I poked at the poinsettia again and watched the chameleon grip more tightly. It trembled. It looked so afraid that I became less afraid. Steeling myself, I lightly stroked its back with my finger. Both eyes swung upward, scanning my finger. The feel of its skin — dry and raspy like emery cloth — surprised me. I brought my face down only a few inches from its face. The pale green neck sagged in a V under its chin. The dark green lips stretched into a painful grin, pinned back at the corners.

Carefully I pinched the creature between my forefinger and thumb. Then I lifted, feeling it clutch at the poinsettia leaf until forced to let go and swim away in the air. Under the loose skin, I could make out tiny muscles moving and tiny parts trying desperately to find a new balance, a new stability.

I placed the chameleon on my palm and steadied it with a finger. It rolled one eye at my face. It rolled the other toward the poinsettia plant, looking both ways at once. I laughed. This was a wonderful, funny creature — too interesting to let go of.

The minute details of the tiny reptile secured me in the present — in Debre Birhan, a small town on the plateau north of Addis Ababa, Ethiopia. America was already fading out of my memory. I could no longer picture my bedroom in Saint Joseph, Missouri, or Grandmother Clara's little bungalow in Hiawatha, Kansas. I couldn't even conjure up Grandmother's face, except for her halo of white hair and a set of teeth laced with silver. My past had dimmed into a hazy cluster of memories more like dreams than reality — a shaft of sunlight on a gingham blanket, a suffused warmth on my skin. But this grotesque little being, with its stiff, unstable legs and spinning eyes, felt very familiar as I balanced it on my palm, tickled by its two-pronged grip. Everything else was vague and distant, but it was solid and green and wonderfully defined. We were both real, the chameleon and me. And so I knew that we belonged together. I would keep it and make it mine.

A Vocabulary for My Senses

AFTER SIX MONTHS at language school in northern Ethiopia, we moved south to our first official mission station. Dad, whose career as a doctor had been on hold, was posted to a hospital near the town of Soddo in Wolaita district. There, we occupied a real house instead of a temporary apartment. The suitcases could stop masquerading as dressers, and though Johnathan was still away at boarding school in Addis Ababa, my younger brother, Nat, was finally old enough to distract me a bit. Plus I had my own yard to gallop in, with grass kept short by a tethered donkey.

Out back, a huge avocado tree spread over the lawn and formed a wonderful leafy world unto itself. Though barely four, I found that I was able to clamber up inside the green dome of leaves. Once there — where heavy limbs reached out parallel to the ground — I prowled in secret, like my pet chameleon, holding thinner branches as handrails. From hidden perches, I monitored the whole mission compound, seeing into the countryside all around.

The Wolaita region was lush compared to the cold, grassy highlands of Debre Birhan. Farm plots covered the terrain, stitched together in green-and-yellow squares and rectangles and trapezoids, blanketing the valleys and even the gentle, sloping mountains. Banana trees with leaves as big as elephant ears flourished behind each thatched house. Papaya trees shot skyward too, looking like poles that had sprouted green footballs.

A red dirt road split the fifteen acres owned by the mission. To the south, where the road entered the compound, four whitewashed classrooms boxed in an open field that served as parade ground and soccer pitch for the mission's elementary school. I could see tin flashing through a row of trees and hear Ethiopian children calling out to each other at recess. Across from these classrooms, a series of long, narrow buildings stretched out in parallel rows, linked by roofed walkways. These were the clinic and patient wards. Made of *chicka* — an Ethiopian adobe of mud and straw and dung — the walls were whitewashed, like all walls on the compound, and the roofs were tin, so they shimmered with silver light at midday. Through the leaves of the avocado I could spy into open windows, where the wooden shutters had been thrown open and patients lay on their iron beds — motionless silhouettes waiting to feel better.

About fifteen missionaries worked at Soddo, and their houses were spread out along the remaining dirt drive. Across from us was the Andersons' squat, block-shaped house, with a spray of banana trees covering one corner. Then came the Schmidts and the Bergens, and the road petered out fifty yards up the slope, where old Selma lived next to her beloved bookshop full of ink-scented gospel tracts and Amharic New Testaments.

I clambered around in the dark foliage of our avocado tree every day, spying on my new world and squeezing the wrinkled fruit to feel its ripeness. Mom made me avocado sandwiches on request, spreading the slick green pulp like butter or adding sliced egg and salt. Then I climbed right back into the tree with half of a sandwich clamped in my mouth, to hide up there under the green umbrella, happily watching the mousebirds as they came and went, pirouetting on their thin tail feathers. I even dreamed at night that I could scramble out on the giant limbs until they bent down and delivered me to lower branches, so that I would slip-slide clear to the ground. Like my chameleon, which I kept in a box full of avocado leaves, I felt safest in a dark green refuge.

The only Ethiopian I encountered daily was Marta the house-worker, with her hair bound up in a blue turban, firm as a soccer ball, and her face turned round by a smile. As she stoked the wood stove and wrung out the wet sheets, she hummed hypnotic tunes. She murmured the same word over and over — *Yesus.*

I felt at ease around Marta, but away from home I became as cautious as my chameleon. If Mom brought me along to fetch Dad from the hospital, I turned my face into her skirts and froze as soon as we entered the waiting room. Dozens of Ethiopian patients were there, perched on wooden benches or lying on the cement floor. These sick strangers with veined wood-smoke eyes and rough skin always wanted to finger my crewcut and cup my arms, as if weighing the soft white flesh. They spat on Nat's corn-silk hair to show their admiration. "*Betam taruno,*" they whispered, as if looking at a remarkable painting or a large diamond. I found these men and women weird and frightening, so I hid and refused to answer questions. I would have preferred they didn't exist.

The avocado tree, the chameleon, the sky: these were my only companions in those first months at Soddo — except for Marta, Nat, and my parents. As a result, what I learned about Ethiopian culture came to me slowly. One morning as Mother planned the Bible lesson she would teach to a women's group, cutting out a cardboard figure of little Zaccheus the tax collector (high in his lookout tree searching for Jesus), she burst out uncharacteristically, "If they wanted us to work with the Wolaita people, then why didn't they teach us Wolaita?"

It had never occurred to me that there were more languages in Ethiopia than the one Mom and Dad had wrestled with at Debre Birhan. Stunned, I asked, "Mama, don't they speak Amharic?"

She sighed. "Only a few. And not the women."

Because of this language gap, Mom often had trouble communicating with Marta. She would bite her lips in exasperation as she tried to pantomime yet another foreign task, such as how to mix the ingredients for an angel food cake — beating the egg whites until they were stiff enough to stand, then adding sifted flour and confectioners' sugar bit by bit.

She became so desperate about managing Marta that she resorted to a pictograph drawn in colored pencil. First she rendered our kitchen clock with an oversize hand pointing to nine; then she drew in the iron stove with red flames blazing from its open door, implying that Marta should refuel it. She paired clock hands pointing to ten with a blue-checkered dress over a basin of sudsy water: time for laundry. Then she drew pots and pans on the stove and a clock with both hands pointing to noon. Lunch!

When Dad came home from the hospital, he too seemed befuddled at times.

"I had a man jump out a window today," he announced one afternoon.

"Charles!" Mom gasped. "He didn't!"

"Headfirst. When I told him I needed to take blood for a transfusion, he dove and ran."

Curious as always, I broke in: "But, Daddy, why would you take his blood?"

"To give to his wife who lost a lot in surgery."

"Then why did he run away?"

Dad grimaced. "Now that's the million-dollar question. Maybe he thought I was going to steal his soul."

"That's crazy," I replied.

Mom chastised me. "Timmy, don't say crazy."

"Mom's right," Dad added. "People die if they lose too much blood, so some of the people in Soddo may think that their spirits live in their blood."

My picture of Ethiopia was my parents' picture, except for rare, weird glimpses stolen from the safety of my crow's-nest high in the avocado tree. Sometimes, when I had found the right roost, I would spy on incoming patients. A group of farmers came along, walking two abreast with their callused toes splayed as they strained under a stretcher of eucalyptus poles and strapped cloth. The woman they carried, pregnant and weary to death, lay buried under white cotton shawls. Only her hands showed, clamping the poles of the litter in a clawlike grip. All I could hear, besides the muffled footfalls in the dust, was her labored breathing, which came out in sudden moaning bursts like air forced from a bellows.

They passed, then along came a blind man led by a little girl, who held onto the opposite end of his staff, guiding him down the road. They went very slowly because his legs were swollen up as thick as an elephant's legs and covered with bloody bandages.

Then came a boy a bit older than me, maybe even the age of my brother Johnathan, who swung himself along on a single T-shaped crutch. The leg next to the crutch ended above the knee in a brown stump. When he stopped and looked up, he spotted me. He just stood there and gawked with an open-mouthed smile.

I had seen this boy lurching by our house before, and I imagined he attended the mission's elementary school where Mom taught English classes. I had overheard Dad muttering once, "All they had to do was to bring him to us!"

He meant the words for Mom, who was standing next to him carving a loaf of bread, but I blurted out, "Who didn't bring him?"

So Dad explained. The boy had fallen out of a tree and broken his leg, but the healer in his village insisted no one should go to the foreign doctors. He splinted the leg himself, tying the splints so tightly the blood couldn't flow. The boy's leg didn't improve; on the contrary, it began to smell like dead fish.

"He had gangrene," Dad said. "And once you get gangrene, there's nothing anyone can do, except cut away the ruined part."

"You cut off his leg?"

"We had to . . ."

"But, Timmy," Mom interrupted, and she adopted her Sunday school voice, "do you see how he smiles? He learned about Jesus while he was here. That's why he comes back so much."

Now, as I stared down from the avocado tree, the crippled boy waved. I put my finger over my lips. He put his own finger over his lips. I pointed down the road, meaning for him to go on. He gestured back the same way, pointing as if I should walk away from my perch into midair. Then I laughed, unable to help myself, and he laughed too. He pivoted on his crutch and swung away, still smiling that enigmatic smile.

• • •

The Wolaita Christians, all of them, had this "something" that the boy had, something that I didn't have and that not even Mom and Dad had, despite all their spiritual yearning. They seemed to carry secret springs inside themselves that bubbled over even in the throes of pain. When evening descended, they would comfort each other by breaking into spontaneous song, chanting strange antiphonal tunes that quavered in minor keys, tender to my unaccustomed ears.

"*Yesus* was poor," the lead singer called out in a tremulous voice, letting the words lift high into the dim, tin-covered rafters of the hospital ward.

"*Yesus* was poor," all the other patients chanted back.

"We are poor too," he sang, and they echoed, "We are poor too."

"But God took care of *Yesus*."

"Yes, God took care of *Yesus*," they replied.

"And God will take care of us . . ."

Sometimes the lead singer made up new verses—"*Yesus* was lonely. We are lonely too." Or "*Yesus* was sick. We are sick too." On and on he went, and the other patients faithfully followed, lying back in their metal cots, full of aches and pains but chanting out this strange, sweet trust.

Their voices drifted out the paneless windows of the mud-walled hospital and across the red dirt road, hanging in the lowering dark, then wafting through our screen door on the evening breeze. The sound drifted through the dimming rooms of our house, then out the back door into the dusky yard and the shadowed avocado tree. I felt something deeply holy about such words and music, even though I understood so little.

At this hour, Dad would also go out and start the generator in the little shed across the road. He yanked at the cord of the antique machine until slowly, patiently, it pumped to life, puttering like the submerged motor on a trawler. This faithful engine, after it had steadied itself on its oil-stained cement pad, settled into a deep thumping rhythm—*pucka, pucka, pucka, pucka*—and I always thrilled at the sound. With it came electricity, the invisible stuff that snaked its way into the house through wires to wake up all the light bulbs.

What a wonderful consistent sound — the pumping of that sturdy old generator. It was time itself, moving predictably, not rushed or spastic. It meant a range of calm things. It meant the coming of the night. It meant the Southern Cross already bright on the horizon. It meant the moon.

Sometimes, Mother would heat the cast-iron kettle on the wood stove and scrub me down in the kitchen. She plopped me into a galvanized washtub next to my brother Nat. If the water went cold, she pulled us out like laundry that needed to be rinsed. Then she added scalding water from the kettle, stirred it a bit, and lifted us back in, to be deliciously warmed.

I could hear the distant tremolo of the singing patients over the pumping of the generator, and I sang my own unconscious song — *Jesus was a child too, just like me. But God took care of Jesus, and God will take care of me.*

I fooled around, tickling Nat, because I knew that if we could prolong the whole wet and slippery process until nine o'clock, the generator would be turned off to save fuel. Then the two of us boys might get dried off in the warm, yellow light of a candle, which was magical in its own way. Maybe we could even escape Mom's grip to race through the flickering house, chasing our giant shadows. If we could just keep her in a good mood, then we might get one last minute of abandonment, delirious with our own clean skin and wet hair.

Eventually, though, we were captured. We went to our beds and said our prayers, mindful to include Johnathan at Bingham Academy and Sisoni Odeiki, the Indonesian orphan we sponsored through World Vision. I thought of the crippled boy too, whose name I did not know. "Lord, take care of the boy with one leg, and everybody else in the whole world. In Jesus' name, amen."

Then I did what all children must do: I went to sleep and grew older.

The Letters She Wrote

I WOKE EARLIER than usual and stepped down onto the cold parquet. I tiptoed to the doorway, looking down the hall and shivering. Mom — still in her terry bathrobe — was seated on one of our cloth armchairs, the orange ones with the Z-shaped, wooden arms. She had her Bible in her lap and she was holding out a green plastic cup as if she had forgotten it was in her hand.

I rubbed the crust out of my eyes and watched. Mom was right there in front of me, but she was also *not* there. She had withdrawn into contemplation, as if she had dropped down into the well of herself and decided to stay there instead of climbing back to the surface where she could look out on the world. Though she faced the big window that framed Mount Damoto, and though the distant ridge was burnished by the morning sun, I could tell she was not aware of any of it. Not the faraway ridge. Not her reflection in the glass. Not me.

Marta cracked a few twigs in the kitchen and blew into the iron stove, but I didn't move because that would be like breaking a spell; Mom might shatter. She was talking to God, and I knew better than to bother her at such a moment. But what kind of talk was going on? What was she saying? What was God saying?

She rotated her head a few degrees toward me, and her eyes slowly filled with awareness. She looked over my shoulder at the

22

wooden clock with the brass hands. Suddenly she was all motion — rising out of the chair, swinging the coffee cup to a side table, plunking the Bible down. "Is it already that late? Timmy, you need to get some clothes. Just grab jeans and a T-shirt. I've got to run to the staff meeting."

When Mom needed to be purposeful, she could become a human dynamo. By the time I had changed into clothes and come to the kitchen, she was fully dressed, pulling at her hair with a brush and trying, in broken Amharic and pantomimes, to make Marta understand that I should be fed while she went to the meeting. She held up two fingers for Marta, explaining that there would be not one but *hulet* guests for breakfast. Cereal water needed to be boiled and mixed with powdered milk. Toast needed to be heated in the oven of the cast-iron stove. Marta should start the primus for extra coffee. And so on.

Thirty minutes later and she was back, bringing two visiting ministers from Canada. These men were fascinated with every aspect of Ethiopian culture. They wanted to know whether it was

MOM IN THE GARDEN AT SODDO.
Rabbit hutches. Mount Damoto too.

true that Amharic had no word for *no*. They asked, "Do the people really believe that Emperor Selassie is descended from Sheba and King Solomon? Is that why all the Coptic churches have their own replicas of the Ark of the Covenant?"

Mom smiled brightly and offered intelligent answers as she shuttled bread and guava jam from the pantry. She juggled my waking brother on her hip and found him a cup with oatmeal while describing the legendary tunnel that supposedly ran all the way from Solomon's palace to the ancient Sabaean kingdom in northern Ethiopia. She described stone palaces that still stood in the northern provinces, along with huge stone steles from 500 B.C., erected and inscribed to commemorate military victories.

The Canadian ministers could tell how much Mom loved this mix of legend and history, with its connection to the Old Testament and God's chosen people. They rose to the occasion, asking more questions, so she continued. She told how two Syrian boys from the fourth century A.D. had survived a pirate raid off the coast of Ethiopia and were brought to the Emperor of Aksum, ruler of the most powerful city-state in northern Ethiopia. She explained how the Emperor appointed one of those slaves, a Christian, as the tutor to his son, and how that prince converted, turning the whole kingdom to Christianity. She told them about the coins archaeologists had found in Aksum—how their imprint changed in the fourth century from the pagan symbols of a sun and moon to a cross.

The men ate heartily and kept Mom talking, and as soon as they left for their tour at a local church, she sighed deeply. The electricity in her smile waned. She threw wood into the iron stove and instructed Marta—with more pantomimes, weary hands in the air—to bake bread before supper. On this day she had to lead a parenting class for new mothers, so there was no stopping for her. She couldn't talk to me. I would have to find something to do. She put a pan in the playpen with Nat and handed him a wooden spoon as a drumstick. She gave me crayons and a coloring book of biblical heroes. If I didn't want to color, I could play in the yard, but only in the yard, not down to the hospital or school. Did I understand?

Then off she scooted, turning up her energy as she stepped out the door with a poster on breastfeeding and an egg timer to show women how long they should devote to each feeding. "See you in a bit, Timmy. You can play with the garden tools but only in the dirt at the edge of the garden. OK?"

I was surprised when she slipped up beside me later in the morning and sat down. I was at the edge of the garden, as instructed, digging with a hand spade.

"No ants in your trousers?" she asked, lifting my cuffs and rubbing my ankles. "That's a very deep hole. Where are you going?"

"I'm gonna hide in it."

"Sounds fun," she said. "You know, when I was little, my brother and I used to dig really long holes, like ditches. We covered them up with boards and dirt, so we could hide too. No one could find us."

I kept digging and she sat there by me, waiting. I thought she would get up and do something about lunch or go to another meeting, but she just stayed there; when I finally looked at her, she was staring across our garden toward the little coop where we kept chickens for eggs. A hen bobbed out the open door of the cage, turned around, bobbed back in. It came out, went in. It stopped on the threshold and pecked halfheartedly at the dirt, and Mom stared, gone again, down into the well of herself.

"Well . . ." she said finally, becoming conscious that I had stopped digging and was watching her, "I'd better get ready for lunch, don't you think?" And she sighed again, lifting herself off the grass, dusting off the back of her flowered skirt.

Mom seemed happier later, after we had all taken our afternoon nap. I woke to a familiar clacking sound and slipped into her bedroom to watch her thumping at the small manual typewriter. When she saw me, she smiled, as though she had just refueled. She pulled three sheets out of the typewriter, separated by carbon paper, and when she peeled them apart, the lettering on the copies had a fuzzy, temporary look to it, floating on the page like blue dust.

"What does it say?" I asked. She didn't answer at first because she was proofreading, so I asked again: "Mama, what's it about?"

She stopped reading and looked at me for a long moment, smiling again.

"It's just about life here in Ethiopia. About the way we live. So our friends back home can imagine it all."

"What sorts of things?"

"Things like the hole you were digging to hide in."

"Nuh-huh."

"Yes, sir. See right here. 'Found Timmy in the garden after class. He was digging a hole. Said he was going to hide in it. Almost joined him.' "

"What other stuff?"

"Just normal things — like how we cook and wash, and how the horse mows the lawn, and how we keep ants out of the sugar."

"How do we keep them out?"

"Haven't you noticed? I always put water in a saucer, then put the sugar bowl in that water. Ants don't like to swim."

"And what else?"

She sighed. "Timmy, it's not for kids."

"But I want to know."

So she told me about the Ethiopian calendar, which had been made long, long ago, and was so different from the American calendar that we were in 1959, not 1965. She told me too about the custom of branding children on the temple with a heated rod — to cure eye disease — or putting cow manure in a person's hair as a kind of stiff hairdress. She told me about a man she called a "witch doctor," saying that he had allowed his sick wife to come to the mission hospital, and when she recovered, he was so impressed that he went home to burn all his relics and evil medicine.

But she also told me there were some people here who wouldn't give up their old religion, even though there was evil and fear in what they believed. She said one man had burned his son on the arm when the boy became a Christian. How? I asked, but she wouldn't tell me. She just said we needed to pray for such people.

That's why she was writing the letter: so everyone back home in America would pray for that man who burned his son.

That afternoon Dad unexpectedly showed up from the hospital with a guest who had just arrived: a Wolaitan evangelist who had gone to America for several months and recently returned. Mom was excited to have this man, Markeena, in our house. She had always talked of him fondly, saying how patiently he translated for missionaries and how cheerful he remained even when he had typhoid and nearly died. Now he was back from where we used to live, and she wanted to know how our country seemed to him.

"I can say it is amazing. I am telling you the truth, Miss Kay, it is not like anything I have seen."

"Did you feel welcomed?"

"Absolutely. I was blessed."

"Were you surprised by anything? It's not all good. We know that."

He hesitated, and then he said, "Miss Kay, I can say only one thing. In some churches, I am sad because maybe they have lost the first love. They are lost, it seems. Here in Wolaita, we are learning from Americans. At our Bible school there are so many books by Americans, too many to count really. But there, in U.S., some churches are sleeping, I think."

Mom sighed and patted her chest. Then Markeena redirected the conversation. He asked, *"Agarachinin lumadoo?"* — meaning "Are you accustomed to our country now?"

She began to answer *"Lumajallo, gin . . ."* or "I am accustomed, but . . ." Then she began to pat at her chest again, and she brushed her wrist across her cheek and retreated into the kitchen where I was watching next to Nat's playpen.

Dad felt the awkwardness of the moment and turned the conversation once more, asking Markeena if he had noticed the influence of the radio in America. He began to explain the difference between rock and roll and classical music. He put a record onto the battery-powered phonograph to demonstrate. It was one of Mom's favorites: a Rachmaninoff concerto she always talked about hearing in Saint Joseph, Missouri, back when she used to take the train to her weekly ballet lessons.

As the piano entered in over the sweeping strings, lingering at the end of each little run, I turned around toward Mom, who was leaning over one of her carbon-copied letters with a pen in her hand, jotting down a change of some sort. The piano rippled with drama and emotion. Mom looked out the back window at the hen, still strutting beside its wire coop. She gazed at it, lost in thought. Then she tore her eyes away and looked down at the letter again. She wrote a few more words.

"What does it say?" I asked.

"It's a verse, Timmy. It's a verse that your Dad and I learned all the way back in America — that helped us to decide to come to Ethiopia. It's from a letter Paul wrote to the people of Rome, when he was a missionary: 'I am debtor both to the Greeks, and to the Barbarians; both to the wise, and to the unwise. So, as much as in me is, I am ready to preach the gospel to you that are at Rome also.'"

She took in a large, shivery breath and she spoke again, but it seemed like she was talking to herself, not me. She said, "Do you know that *gospel* means 'good news'? Well, Jesus can't be good news unless we share him. That's why Markeena went to America, and that's why we came here to Soddo."

She folded the letter and put it into an envelope and sealed it. She set it on the kitchen table. Then she went back into the living room carrying a fresh pot of tea and sugar.

The Emperor's Smile

WE HAD NOT BEEN at the Soddo station very long when a rumor began. It was confirmed later by a letter that arrived at the hospital: Emperor Haile Selassie would be paying a visit to our region. He would come in April, after the harvest was through.

Suddenly, all the townspeople of Soddo began preparing, as if his Highness might come into each home to eat and take his coffee. I could see the changes when I rode with Dad to town for supplies at the market. People were repairing the thatched roofs on their *tukels*. They were patching cracked walls with *chicka,* stomping together mud and straw and cattle dung to make fresh batches of the dark adobe. At the center of town they had whitewashed every wall that faced the street. A few shop owners were even using expensive enamel paint to coat their shops in slick blue.

The official word was that the Emperor would grace Soddo with a royal banquet, and this meant that building a banquet hall had become imperative. A work crew tackled the project. They bordered a grassy field with whitewashed rocks. They raised a wide tin roof on wooden posts, leaving the dry-season grass spread out like a tan rug underneath. Then they erected an arch of poles, decorating the peeled eucalyptus with sashes of green and yellow and red — the colors of the Ethiopian flag.

I saw the newly erected structure when my father drove me and

Emperor Haile Selassie greeted by mission staff at Soddo station.

Mom and baby Nat into the market on market day. After we had squeezed through a gauntlet of vendors, sidestepping stacks of rat traps and matches and bricks of yellow soap, I escaped onto Soddo's wide parade ground and ran toward the new hall. A cluster of local kids followed, all trying out their English phrases — "Whaddis your name? Please, my friend?" — but I ignored them. I passed under the tall arch of eucalyptus poles that billowed with sashes of cloth. Where the bent poles met, there hung a painting of the Lion of Judah, proud symbol of the Emperor. Even though I was too young to understand fully, I felt the raw power of the image, felt it in my bones. The son of the son (a dozen times over) of Solomon. A true king. A biblical king.

In the banquet hall, a group of Wolaitan children, still in their blue school uniforms, were practicing the national anthem. Their voices crescendoed and held at fortissimo. They trumpeted the concluding verse, singing in the official state language of Amharic. Then they spilled out of the building, firing off snatches of the memorized lyrics, so that the anthem faded away down the dirt paths, twisting through the woods and across the fields, set loose.

Dad called to me and I had to go back to the Land Rover, but that Amharic song had stuck with me, and it was reinforced during the next two weeks when I heard children practicing in the countryside. The words drifted down out of the hills above our mission station and wandered in the woods below our house. The song seemed to seep right out of the soil or lower from the sky:

> Etyopia, hoy! Dess ye-bellish
> Be-Amlakish hile be-Negusish
> Tebaberowal inah arbignochish . . .

At evening it was still quavering in the distance, where children rehearsed it as they gathered the goats and chickens, corralling them inside their thatched houses.

> O Ethiopia, sing out your joy
> In the power of your God and king,
> United with your ancestors, brave and true . . .

With nightfall the song quieted, muffled by the thatch and the darkness, but I imagined children still murmuring it as they settled in by the night fires with the sleepy animals warming the air at their backs. I imagined them singing in their sleep.

When the longed-for day came at last, Haile Selassie displayed his royal favor toward us as foreigners by appearing at our mission compound within hours of his arrival. Dad rushed out of the hospital along with the other staff — the white doctors and nurses and the Ethiopian dressers — who stood at attention next to a row of Ethiopian flags. Since I had heard the convoy coming, I was already up in my avocado tree, peeking through the leaves. I recognized the Emperor before he climbed out of his jeep. I had seen him in the black-and-white photograph that appeared in the hospital waiting room, positioned higher than the anatomy charts and Bible illustrations. In person, he was surprisingly short but handsome. He exuded royalty, dressed neatly in a khaki uniform, his left shoulder and breast covered with ribbons and medals. His peppery hair was topped with a cap that would have made any air force pilot proud. His receding hairline gave him a high, dignified fore-head. And his hawklike nose made him seem slightly dangerous.

As I watched the Emperor saluting my father with the flags whipping overhead, I knew I had seen something to boast about. I couldn't wait for my older brother to return from boarding school. What news! The Lion of Judah himself.

However, I lost some of my enthusiasm when Mom called me down out of the tree and straitjacketed me into my Sunday best. That meant a scratchy white shirt pressed into stiffness by an iron hot from the wood stove. I had to wear a bow tie too, and very shiny black leather shoes. A little tan suit coat, with a badge on the breast pocket, completed the outfit. This badge — boasting a crown and crossed swords — had probably been sewn there to lure me into the jacket, which I avoided on every occasion.

Mom put Nat into a casual short-sleeved shirt, which looked unfairly comfortable. However, she also wrestled him into pow-der-blue, suspendered pants that only a two-year-old could wear, which made me feel better. Dad came home and walked me to the Land Rover. Mom carried Nat, who arched his back and whined. Then we drove to the Soddo parade grounds, where we would be official guests at the Emperor's banquet.

I doubt my parents expected any further special treatment, but to their amazement, the Emperor had assigned us to a table quite close to his dais, a white wooden platform with a series of steps. We took our places at metal folding chairs, arranged around a wooden table with an actual linen tablecloth. Only ten yards away and six or eight feet higher than us sat the Emperor, calmly watch-ing as his meal of *injera ba wat* was set out for him.

"Charles, do you think they've made a mistake?" Mom whis-pered.

He looked back at her silently, with the impassive, unsmiling face that meant he was nervous.

Mom turned to me. "Timmy, do you see the Emperor?" she whispered. "Aren't we lucky to sit so close."

I took my cue from Dad, saying nothing.

I had noticed that even though people were murmuring, their attention seemed pinned on the Emperor, who sat up there all alone. I had never seen so many people so vigilant. I grew silent. When he dipped his *injera* into the spicy stew, I followed suit, but I ate with unusual concentration, too busy chewing to appreciate the soft sourdough taste of the *injera* or the extra-fine medley of spices in the three kinds of *wat*. Dad gave me one of the hard-boiled eggs from the *doro wat,* normally my favorite morsel, but I picked at it without relish.

A boy my own age crept up outside the hall and pressed his face against the lattice of eucalyptus poles. Flies scurried around his sticky nose. He didn't brush them off. This spectacle was too amazing for such distractions — first the Emperor on his throne, then us albino people eating from a table with a cloth so white it might have been woven from clouds.

Suddenly, a craggy old man appeared and lashed the boy's bare legs with a switch. The child turned and ran, scattering flies.

"*Woosha,*" muttered the guard, using the Amharic term for "Dog!" He stalked along the eucalyptus divider, menacing any children who dared to peek through the slats.

Alarmed, I risked a quick sweep of the hall, taking in the hefty Ethiopian lords with their tan linen jackets and the sturdy ladies in exquisite white dresses with embroidered hems and scarves — a sea of white and tan and blue, decorated with bands of red and green and gold. That's when I realized that Nat and I were the only children here under the roof. Being *ferengis* apparently gave us permission to break the rules that kept other children outside — even the ones dressed in their newly washed and ironed school uniforms, waiting to sing the national anthem.

Now I wished that I could become invisible like my pet chameleon. However, to my horror, I became more noticeable.

By the Emperor's feet lay a Chihuahua. Lulu was another of Haile Selassie's trademarks, and she traveled everywhere with him. Recently she had been to Washington, D.C.; Mom had read about it from a newspaper clipping her friends sent from Kansas

City. Lulu looked small but quite regal, and when I saw her lounging at the feet of the Emperor, I knew she had to be important. I was dismayed when, without warning, she leapt up from her napping position and rushed down the steps of the dais right to our table.

This royal Chihuahua slipped under the white linen tablecloth and began to growl. I lifted the cloth to discover her right at my feet, staring straight at me. Then she began to bark. On and on she went — yapping in that shrill, frantic way that only Chihuahuas can manage — until everyone in the great hall went silent and craned their necks to see what was wrong. I could feel their gaze sliding all over my white face and straight black hair, over my shiny leather shoes and tan jacket and the little badge with crossed swords and a crown that was sewn on my breast pocket. Paralyzed, I couldn't climb out of my chair or jump to my mother's arms or scream. With so many people watching, anything might be a mistake, so I hiked myself up in the chair and lifted my legs straight out in front of me until my toes pressed the underside of the table.

I glanced at the Emperor. The tiny dog belonged with its master, which meant there was a good chance Haile Selassie would be angry. I peeked again with tears burning in my eyes, and to my amazement the stern little man was no longer stern. He was smiling. He was looking straight at me — this unimportant foreign boy from America — and smiling.

A fierce shriek split the air, and I was forgotten. An Ethiopian warrior with a leopard-skin headdress and a black shield of hippo hide loped down the center aisle of the banquet hall. In his free hand he lifted a lance, aiming right at the Emperor.

"Watch out!" I wanted to shout. I had been shocked out of my misery. But before I could react, the warrior had leapt up the steps to the throne.

The steel tip of the lance stopped just inches from the Emperor's chest. It flickered there, silver and black, dancing in front of the rows of medals. The warrior yowled as though preparing to lunge. Instead of flinching, the Emperor stared straight back, then simply held out his open hand. On his palm lay a copper coin.

The warrior lowered his spear. He bowed. Then he took the coin, spun, and raced back out of the banquet hall. I became aware again of the Chihuahua, which had sprinted back to the royal dais and was barking in an apoplectic frenzy, leaping off its feet with rage.

"Yikes," Father exclaimed, raising his eyebrows in mock terror. Nat and I laughed. This was wonderful entertainment. We'd all been fooled.

I was amused but also nervous. On high alert, animal-like, I think I could sense hidden resentment floating on the breeze that day in 1964 — drifting like a strange scent. Roast garlic. Cumin. Singed hair. Though I could not understand the situation, I felt the presence of unexpressed emotions: perhaps the envy of the Amhara aristocrats who had observed us being seated next to the Emperor, or the anger of the Wolaita serfs who were kept outside the hall, not allowed to join the celebration. The attacking warrior was role-playing, but I sensed danger stored up in his spear, maybe more than even he knew.

In the months to follow, I often dreamed of Haile Selassie. I pictured him always doing the same inscrutable thing — leading me to the lip of a great cliff. I followed cautiously as he swept his arm out over the edge, indicating that his kingdom stretched clear to the horizon. I felt that, for some special reason, he had chosen me to show this to, but I was afraid to look. His cape whipped in the wind. I feared for him because he stood too close to the edge of the cliff. Why did he seem so sad? I asked myself.

He peered down over the edge, but I hung back. Whatever lay beyond seemed too much. Not yet. Not yet. I was only four years old. I was not ready yet to see so much. But I felt called forward, asked to take account.

Birth Order

AS THE RAINY SEASON set in, turning the burned back of Mount Damoto lush green and blanketing the countryside with wet grass, the long holiday of July and August drew near. Mom and Dad mentioned Johnathan more. *In only three weeks your brother will arrive. Just two weeks to go. Ten days now.*

I had not thought of Johnathan much except when we sent him letters. Then I had dictated little asides, letting Mom add them before she folded and sealed the tissuey blue aerograms. I had boasted about seeing the Emperor and climbing clear to the top of the avocado tree. I had also told him about our new pets, two rabbits kept in a chicken-wire box next to the house. They crouched motionless — two balls of black-and-white fluff with glistening black eyes. Watching them produced few results. But if we poked a stick through the chicken wire, they sprang into action, scattering the pile of brown pellets that had collected underneath them.

"You have to come see the bunnies," I dictated for Mom to add to the letter sent just before Johnathan came home on holiday. I waited while Mom penned the words, then I added more: "We named them Sunny and Yum-Yum because Mom tells us stories about rabbits named Sunny and Yum-Yum. We take shrinking pills and ride on their backs. They go down holes to another world."

Mom smiled softly, glad to see my enthusiasm for her bedtime stories. "Do you think Johnathan will like the bunny stories?"

"Yeah. Why don't you tell him he can be in the stories, when he comes."

I felt proud of the turf I had staked out in Soddo, and excited that I would be able to show it to my big brother. Three months had passed since I had last seen Johnathan, and now he seemed like a special guest. When he flew into the Soddo airstrip, stepping down from a bulging silver DC-3, I talked nonstop. At the mission station, I dragged him into the backyard. "Look, there's the avocado tree. I can climb way out on the branches and they don't even break. And that's Mount Damoto, the one that looks like a chameleon's back. And there's Sunny and Yum-Yum. They're both girls."

Johnathan lagged behind, grinning uncertainly, unsure whether to trust what I said. I could tell that he was impressed with the rabbits, however, because he got down with his nose right up to the chicken wire, where the musty fur smell was strongest. Then he asked me which one was Sunny and which was Yum-Yum.

I relished this whole reversal. Here I was, only four, and I could tell this eight-year-old things he didn't know. However, a few days later Johnathan one-upped me. "Hey, everybody, look at this," he called from the front door.

Nat and I were washing hands for supper. We ran to join our brother with Mom and Dad close behind. A heavy rain had just let up and, after the roar on our tin roof, the world seemed wonderfully silent, except for the soft pattering from trees. Two hunters stood on the wet cinders with a live animal the size of a goat slung upside-down between them, its legs strapped to the shaft of a spear. Johnathan reached up to stroke the bristly back, which glistened with raindrops. The creature trembled.

"It's OK," he murmured, stroking the animal, which we all recognized by now as a miniature deer, or dik-dik.

"Can I have it?" Johnathan suddenly burst out. "Please? Because you know they will just kill it."

"It's mine too," I yelped.

"Me too," echoed Nat, standing in his diaper and red rubber boots.

"Boys . . ." Mom cautioned.

The two hunters had not moved an inch, each shouldering one end of the spear and staring over our heads toward Dad, the man of the house. He greeted them in Amharic and launched into a clumsy discussion. The front man, whose hair was slick with rainwater and who wore only shorts, pointed at a dead guinea fowl on the ground. He poked it with his toe, turning the carcass to reveal the bird's elegant pinstriped breast. The other hunter lifted a lean brown hare dangling from a string around his waist. Its matted corpse looked nothing like the fluffy cotton of our pet rabbits.

Johnathan stepped up on the porch now, and reached for Dad's forearm. "I'll take care of the dik-dik myself, I promise. I'm old enough."

"I'm old enough too."

"Boys . . ." repeated Mom. "It's not a contest . . ." She looked to Dad for a decision.

"*Please* . . ." Johnathan and I chorused, with Nat echoing.

"All right," Dad said. "Since Johnathan is home from school. But you'll have to take good care of it. Do you understand?" And he gave Johnathan a stern glance.

The next day, Tusuma, our part-time gardener, wove a low fence of split bamboo and staked it into the ground as a corral. Johnathan and I argued over who would be first to go inside the corral to feed the tiny deer. "*Madoqua*," we called it, which was Amharic for "dik-dik." When I held the baby bottle, I sang to the deer, and it bumped my chest with tiny horns: gray nubs no bigger than a fingertip. I thrilled with each contact, relishing its rough hide under my palm, its raspy tongue nibbling the milk on my fingers, its sharp hooves kneading my thighs — until Johnathan demanded the bottle back.

Johnathan and I often interacted like that, in a kind of competitive tug of war. He would initiate some new activity, and I would grab hold of the idea, pulling it my direction. Having him home from boarding school had changed the whole configuration of the family. I was no longer the oldest son, the one setting the pace. I wanted to prove that I was just as mature. However, measuring myself against a much older boy, I kept falling short.

Of course Nat, who was now walking and talking, wanted attention too. But Johnathan's grand plans seemed more appealing, so I turned away from Nat, leaving him uncharacteristically grouchy.

Johnathan begged to go to the stream with Tusuma. Even though we had plenty of drinking water, collected from the downspouts during the daily rains, Tusuma went to the stream every few days to water the donkey or bring back extra water for the laundry. Eventually, Mom gave in, and since I could manage that hike, she let me go along. Nat, on the other hand, had to remain behind. He writhed in her arms, and after she set him down, he fell back wailing on the grass, cheeks red with emotion.

I trotted beside the donkey, my hand on its warm flank. While Tusuma tipped the five-gallon tins into the river and hoisted them onto the wooden rack that was lashed to the donkey, I followed Johnathan out into the burbling current, feeling for hollows with my soggy shoes or accidentally stepping down to hip depth and reemerging in delighted shock to prance and shiver. Johnathan and I threw stones at water spiders and built little dams, and then we came reluctantly when Tusuma called out, *"Lidgeoch, inaheed"* — "Children, let's go."

It was rainy season, so we were always wet. Since the river felt warmer than the air, we loved to play in it, reaching deep for rocks or cupping tadpoles. But we couldn't always be at the river, and if it kept raining and raining, we grew tired of the wetness, retreating indoors.

Johnathan, focused and organized, had started a stamp collection. Nat and I joined him on his bed as he tore off the corners of envelopes Mom had kept. He soaked these torn corners in saucers of water, peeling away the stamps with tweezers and drying them on a cotton rag. Meanwhile, I acted as official guardian, keeping Nat from grabbing or crumpling.

I watched with fascination as Johnathan slid the dried stamps into the cellophane slip covers in his book, each one providing a cryptic clue to its country of origin: stone ruins from Greece, a mountain road in Argentina, a propeller plane from Spain super-imposed over what looked like one of Columbus's ships, and from Ethiopia a whole array of Coptic crosses and ancient emperors.

Another boy had come back from boarding school on the same plane with Johnathan — the Andersons' son. Sometimes he butted in on our time together, whether it was sorting stamps indoors or playing with Madoqua outside. He and Johnathan both had sling-shots, which made me sick with jealousy. I longed to hold the smooth, peeled Y of my brother's slingshot — to pull back the leather pouch, stretching the yellow surgical tubing. I longed to let fly with a rock. But Johnathan protested if I even looked at the cov-eted weapon. Instead, I was relegated to a distant audience, trail-ing along as he and the Anderson boy stalked their prey — mostly lizards.

These blue-black lizards lounged on large rocks when the sun came out between rains. They lay there like sleeping darts, until someone moved too quickly or loudly. Then they snapped across the boulders and vanished.

Johnathan and the Anderson boy shouted at me that it was my fault. "You got too close!" "You're too loud."

They ran away, ducking around the buildings on the mission compound and doubling back, and eventually I ended up alone, wandering the backyards of the other mission houses, hot and sticky under the sweltering sun. Like Nat, I sat down on the damp grass or lay back and stared straight up at the dense white-and-gray clouds that sailed by like ships in the sky. I tracked them until they disappeared in procession behind the green hump of Mount Damoto.

I had lost my pet chameleon before Johnathan came home for vacation. One day when I shuffled through the curling leaves in its box, it wasn't there. I had lost it before, only to discover it climbing the gold-and-green drapes in the living room. This time, however, I couldn't find it even after I searched the house three times over.

Now, as I lay alone in the Andersons' yard, watching the drifting clouds, a tiny motion caught my eye. I turned my head to see a dark chameleon in a nearby shrub. It could be mine, I thought, although it seemed an inch or two longer and more vivid — almost blue-green.

I stared at the chameleon, considering whether to get up and pull it off the shrub. I stared at it so long that I let go of the idea. I liked that it was out here in the bushes where it belonged. If it really was mine, I liked knowing that I had found it again. I was the only one who had been quiet enough and attentive enough to see it.

A fly landed on the branch in front of the chameleon, and I stared as the fly moved closer. Almost never had I seen my pet catch a moving fly, since usually I fed it bugs that I had killed with a swatter. Now, I studied this uncaptured chameleon as the fly brushed its face with its front legs, squatted as if preparing to sleep, and — *zap* — disappeared.

The tongue of the chameleon had retracted so quickly it was hard to believe it had been extended. The chameleon hadn't even shifted. Only its jaws moved, shutting slowly, like a vice, as the fly flailed on the sticky muscle. Everything about the creature was stealthy — even its eating. I would leave it here, unnoticed. Let Johnathan and the Anderson boy pursue their lizards. The chameleon would be *my* secret.

Bushwhacking

ONE AFTERNOON DURING the month before Johnathan went back to boarding school, Dad proposed a trip. It would be a special trip just for him and Johnathan and me. He said he had to deliver diesel fuel to another station one hundred kilometers away — a half-day journey on dirt roads. In honor of Johnathan finishing his first year at school, he would take the two of us boys along. Nat wasn't old enough, but I qualified.

What excitement! To ride anywhere in the Land Rover meant adventure, and I knew from what Dad had told me that the road to Bolosso was a full of surprises. Out there in the "bush," each set of ruts made its own way around puddles and rocks and trees. Riding in the Land Rover would be like riding an unbroken horse, replete with bucking, bottom-slapping action.

On the day before we left, I watched with fascination as Dad filled the jerry cans, siphoning the diesel out of a reserve barrel and spewing the acrid stuff from his mouth when it shot down the hose too quickly. He latched the tall, rectangular cans into racks above the bumpers of the Land Rover, then tied two more onto the roof rack, where they sloshed heavily. Food was packed for the trip: avocado sandwiches, hardboiled eggs, and a priceless can of sardines. A message was sent by short-wave radio to alert the other mission station we were on our way, bringing fuel.

We went to bed, but I couldn't sleep. Even though Mother threatened to spank me, I couldn't shut my eyes or quit wiggling. I paddled my feet under the blankets until she pinned them. How could I not be excited, knowing that in a few hours I would launch on a genuine adventure, not a make-believe fantasy but a real, adult expedition? Just me, Johnathan, and Dad.

All too soon Mom was rubbing my sluggish head and sliding clothes onto my stiff limbs. Then Dad was carrying me in the pre-dawn dark to the Land Rover. He set me down on the cold plastic seat next to Johnathan, who held his slingshot in his lap, yawning and scratching at his rumpled crest of brown curls. Dad got in and turned the key. The engine coughed. It seemed loud and rude in the early morning silence. Mom looked alarmed.

"Charles," she asked, "are you sure you don't want to take another man along?"

"Are you questioning my adequacy as a driver, as a provider, as a Bascom?"

She smiled. "You know what I mean. What if . . ."

"No problem!" Dad interjected. "I've got the boys. If I run into trouble, we'll get out of it. Right, boys?"

"Right!" we sang, quick on our cue.

"Men!" Mom exclaimed in mock caution, lifting one eyebrow, and I thrilled to be included in her adult description.

Dad expresses some Land Rover frustration.

"Relax," he added. "It's all under control."

Mom kept her eyebrow raised, although she couldn't help smiling as she replied, "All right, but be sure to call by short-wave as soon as you get there."

"Ten-four," Dad replied, and he let out the clutch, easing the Land Rover onto the dusky red road that ran through the mission station.

Mother blew a kiss. We all blew kisses back, and Dad called out the window, "Look for us by supper tomorrow, God willing."

Usually the mission road would be crowded with people, but this early in the morning it was empty. The windows of the hospital were dark, and everything seemed abandoned. Even Dad must have been affected by the vacancy of the station because, when he pointed us down the hill to the stream that ran behind our compound, he broke the silence with a jocular "Tally ho."

The Land Rover gathered speed. Trees flashed past, dark green in the morning light. We went faster and faster—too fast in fact. Because the brakes had failed.

Dad kicked at the floor and ground the gears, wrestling to keep the swaying vehicle upright. We barely made the last curve on the steep, twisted road, with the overhead jerry cans pulling us sideways. The Land Rover swooshed through the stream at the bottom of the valley, then bumped up the other bank. When we finally stopped, Dad leapt out and lunged for a large rock. He shoved it behind one of the back wheels.

"Lord, Lord, Lord," we could hear him whisper.

The next day—with the brakes bled and repaired—we were off again.

"Charles, are you sure you should still take the boys?" Mom asked.

"When you get thrown off the horse, you gotta get back on. Right, guys?"

"Right!" we called out.

This time the brakes held, and we drove through Soddo town

without incident, continuing west on a dirt road that had dried out as the rains eased up over the last week. Our destination was still the McClellans' station, which lay near the great Omo River in an area that was cut off from the outside and much less traveled. I had never taken a trip so far away from our new home. For a while, however, the terrain looked familiar. On the other side of Soddo we bumped past a huge tree that I had seen before. Ridged and knuckled, the wide trunk gripped the ground tightly then rose to the height of a man and branched out in gigantic limbs. This muscular, multibranched trunk supported a wide canopy of leaves, more thick and inviting than even the leaves of my avocado. The last time we had passed by, I had noticed sheaves of grain stacked by the base, and a few large red clay pots. This time, a goat stood there, tethered to a stake.

"Somebody forgot their goat," I yelled over the rumble of the engine.

"A what?" Dad yelled back. He had poor hearing already, though only thirty-five.

"A goat!"

Johnathan and I both pointed back toward the giant tree.

"That's a sacrifice," Dad yelled. "For the tree god."

"Is there really a god in there?" I asked, imagining swirling vapor and a whispered voice.

"Don't be stupid," Johnathan shouted back.

Dad shook his head and grinned. "It's just their way of trying to understand things. When bad stuff happens they think someone's angry. They don't know who, so they imagine a tree god or a river god, or another one. Then they give it sacrifices."

"But you're not supposed to give sacrifices, are you?"

"Duh," muttered Johnathan.

"You've got it," said Dad reaching over to tousle my hair. "Nobody needs sacrifices after what Jesus did."

The farther we went, the worse our road became, until it was hard to pick out from the local cattle trails and farm paths. Sometimes it split altogether, forcing us to check the compass on the dashboard. Creaking, the Land Rover climbed in and out of ravines. It slipped into ruts and ground along like it had lost its wheels. Then it skipped back up onto higher ground, shuddering. The trip didn't seem as much fun as earlier, and I tired from the constant rocking and jostling.

Finally we jerked to a halt, blocked by a flooded river that was surging with red, silty water. The recent rains had swept away the bridge. Although a road crew had begun rebuilding it — using wheelbarrows and pickaxes and handcut logs — to wait for them to finish this repair would take months.

Johnathan piped up, "Are we going to have to go back?"

Dad's jaw muscles popped, but he stuck to his script: "What? Bascoms turning back? What would your Granddad say?"

We had heard stories about Grandpa Bascom, whom I could hardly remember at all. He was a doctor like Dad, and he had been raised on a homestead in North Dakota where the nearest tree was seven miles away. His dad — my great-grandfather — had lost a toe in a blizzard while searching for a fence to lead him home. I knew that Grandpa Bascom was old now but that he still liked to ride horses and hunt elk. "You know," Dad said, as we looked out over the flooded river, "once your Granddad got out in a storm and walked across a river up to his waist, just so he could help a sick man on the other side."

It was as if he was trying to convince himself to act. He lifted a fist: "If a man's worth his salt, he doesn't give up." Then he got out of the Land Rover and waded into the river, picking out the ripples around a sandbar, the boil marks that might indicate deep water. He climbed into the cab and pushed the red plunger that would shift us into four-wheel drive. "Hold on," he said, and we jolted forward, all four wheels grabbing at the riverbank.

The sturdy little vehicle clawed through the mud and crept into the silty water. It went on until the current was squeezing in under the doors and spilling across the floorboards. Miraculously, it still crawled forward, sending out a gentle wake.

Johnathan and I shouted with glee. We were doing it. We were practically swimming across this river. Dad grinned.

Then the engine coughed, and Dad muttered, "Please, Lord. Not now. Not here."

But his prayer was in vain. With us halfway across the wide red river, the engine sputtered and died.

Johnathan sensed Dad's anxiety and climbed out on the running board as Dad lifted the hood. He asked, "Do you think you can fix it?"

When Dad didn't answer, he added hopefully, "Maybe if you just wait, then it will work. It could just be a flooded engine, right?"

For Dad, of course, things couldn't be worse: a swamped vehicle in the middle of nowhere and two kids to care for. For me, though, things couldn't be better. We were three desperate castaways in a gray boat, our anchor snagged on the rocks. We were the Swiss Family Robinson gone to Africa. I climbed out on the running board next to Johnathan. I leaned down and scooped up a handful of water, so silty I couldn't see my palm. I straightened up and, unable to resist, I poured it down the nape of Johnathan's neck.

"Cut it out," he yelled, pushing back. With a start, I lost my grip on the door frame and fell into the river, standing up wet to the armpits. I slapped a handful of water onto his legs, he kicked some back, and soon we were engaged in a full water war.

Dad was not amused. This was more than he had bargained for when he decided to include us on the trip. As a four-year-old, I was small enough to be swept away by the current. He shouted for us to get back in the Land Rover, and when we didn't, he collared us both and slung us into the back compartment. We sat there sullenly, stunned by his anger but secretly enjoying the emerging crisis. We were united now. We schemed: How could we get out of here and back into the river?

Dad sloshed to the driver's side and tried unsuccessfully to restart the engine. He got out and slammed the door. And that's when Johnathan and I noticed the bridge workers, who began laughing and pointing as Dad heaved at the back end of the Land Rover.

These workmen were a fearsome lot, striding around barefoot

and shaggy-haired with knotted muscles in their thighs and arms. They were wiry, bowlegged men with craggy faces. They wore nothing but baggy shorts, which had stretched into permanently distorted shapes from all the bending and squatting.

As Dad climbed back into the driver's seat and sat there staring at the windshield, the bridge crew hoisted a fifteen-foot log and ran it like a battering ram out onto the platform they were building. They tipped the log until it plunged into the river with a splashing *thump*. I knew that Mom would prod if she were here: "Charles, shouldn't we ask those men for help?" But I wasn't going to say anything of the sort.

After a few minutes one of the bridge workers pointed at our Land Rover. He climbed down the bridge pilings onto the riverbank and waved at the others to follow. They seemed to argue with him before he turned and shouted toward us.

"Dad, look!" Johnathan yelled. "What's he trying to say?"

I wasn't sure we really wanted to know. But Dad stepped out into the river and cupped his ear with a hand. He had rotten hearing, and since he still struggled to understand Amharic, he was often shrugging and asking people to try again. Now he waded to the shore, up to his thighs in the swirling river, where the whole bridge crew dropped their tools and gathered around him.

I felt damp and cold. When the spokesman for the bridge workers addressed him, Dad shook his head. They seemed to be arguing about something. However, the other workers didn't even wait to listen. They turned and started wading right toward us.

Dad and the spokesman chased after them, and a few seconds later, they all stood around the Land Rover. The spokesman repeated whatever he had been requesting, and Dad shook his head. I thought I heard the word *mismoor*, a word I had heard at church, a word that meant "song." Did they want a song from my father —here? Now?

Dad couldn't hide a grimace. Anger was tightening the skin around his mouth.

The Ethiopian spokesman waited, rubbing his whiskered face

with a wiry hand. Stalemate. Then he turned to his comrades and gave them an explanatory lecture. They all shrugged, and one of them produced a rope.

Were they going to tie my father up? I wondered. But to my relief, instead they looped the rope around the bumper of the Land Rover and spread out along it. They began to heave at it, stretching toward the far bank. The Land Rover rocked. It rose out of its ruts and began to roll.

"Cool," Johnathan called out.

The men pulled even harder, leaning into the air and taking quick, firm steps. Their feet splashed out of the water. They kept pulling, until at last the wheels emerged. But still they didn't stop, dragging the dead vehicle right up the riverbank onto the road.

Surely they were done now, I thought, but to my delight they started to move faster, until they were trotting, each man gripping the rope with one hand instead of two. Dad ran alongside the rear cab of the Land Rover, where Johnathan and I remained prisoners. He opened a side door, grinning. Then he pulled us out, still galloping, and put us on the hood so we could enjoy the craziness of it all. As we passed a thatched house, dogs barked and rushed through the hedge. They bit at the wheels of the Land Rover, baffled by its silence. Children raced to meet us too, hiding wide-eyed behind tree trunks. They watched our procession pass, then gently waved, assured that we were at a safe distance. Johnathan and I waved back.

The workers ran on, entering a tunnel of trees. I closed my eyes and enjoyed the breeze. I lay back on the hood, and the speckled light flickered across my eyelids. The men began to sing. What an adventure this was turning into — better than anything I could have imagined.

Amazingly, these kind bridge workers pulled us as far as the next village, where Dad thanked them profusely, shaking their hands one at a time as if congratulating an Olympic team. Although he had been reluctant to turn to them, now he was indebted. Money was not the issue; they didn't even ask for payment. But Dad wanted them each to know how much he appreciated their help.

They left at last, jogging smoothly on the dirt road, and that is when we realized we were still stuck. The Land Rover wouldn't start and we were miles from our destination. The only way we could reach the McClellans' station by nightfall was by hiking or riding mules. Father began negotiating with the men of the village who had congregated around the broken vehicle. Eventually, he rented two mules and a donkey. The owner saddled them up, and we set off again.

This was just past the height of the rainy season. Dad had hoped to avoid rain since the skies had been clear for a day or two, but all afternoon the clouds had been turning grayer. Now they blotted out the sun, and it began to rain in earnest.

It was a steady, tropical rain, falling straight down in big drops, splattering on the path. Without wind, there was no sound but the steady *splat* of the raindrops, the grunts of the animals, and the creaking of the saddle girths. Since Mom had thought to pack our rain ponchos, we put those on. Meanwhile, the owner of the animals and his son, who were guiding us on foot, broke off two banana leaves, long as canoes, and carried these over their heads.

For a while, we moved along smoothly, with the rain clouds pressing down overhead, seeming as low as the treetops. The gloomy light made it hard to know whether this was four in the afternoon or a minute before sunset. Then, without warning, my donkey sat down. One moment, I was four feet in the air; the next, my toes were in the mud.

The owner smacked the rump of the donkey. Sluggishly, the animal rose and walked on. But as soon as our guide had gotten back to the head of the convoy to take the reins of the lead mule, my donkey sat down again. The reluctant animal kept plunking down without warning, resting its folded legs in the streaming path, and the owner spent the rest of the trip jogging back to swat it, then running forward to pull at the mules. We went down the winding path in fits — stopping, starting, stopping, starting — until we wondered if we would ever get to the McClellans'.

At last, we could see the house through the gloomy forest— two windows warm with lamplight, two spots of yellow winking between the black tree trunks. "Thank you, Jesus," Dad murmured.

I was shivering as we reined in, drenched by the rain that had saturated my exposed trousers. My bottom ached. My hands were stiff on the saddle horn. And I was tremendously tired. After taking so long to arrive, all I wanted to do was to sleep. We ate and Father lay me down somewhere warm and dry where I sank, without protest, into the depths of rest. I slept so hard I had no dreams. I slept without moving a muscle, as a fish might sleep at the bottom of a lake, heavy with darkness and silence.

When I finally woke, it was midmorning and all the McClellans were laughing downstairs at the breakfast table as Dad recounted our adventure at the river. He still couldn't believe the bridge workers had asked him to sing in exchange for their help.

"What was the word they used?" Mrs. McClellan asked.

"*Mismoor,* or something like that."

Mr. McClellan slapped the breakfast table with delight.

"They didn't want you to sing," he said. "They were asking for nails! They needed nails."

"Story of my life," Dad replied, shaking his head.

Johnathan and I grinned at the McClellans' blond, freckled daughters, happy to have such an adventurous and humorous father. We felt pleasantly important, having worked so hard to come here to this far away corner of Ethiopia. Yet already it was time to go. We had promised Mother we would come back by supper.

The McClellans drove us to the stranded Land Rover, and Mr. McClellan tinkered with it until it hiccupped back to life. Then he cautioned Dad to unhook the fan belt next time he crossed a river, to avoid spraying water on the spark plugs or wiring. Dad shook his head as he listened, humiliated again. He was tugging at a jerry can that had jammed in the rack. Not thinking, he slid a screwdriver between the rack and the canister, and leaned back. *Pfff!* The tip of the screwdriver lanced the aluminum can, so that a stream of diesel shot out — the same diesel that we had driven so far to deliver.

By the time the McClellans had escorted us back to the river — ready to rescue us if need be — Dad was more than ready to say goodbye. He had protested against them coming this far. As he drove the Land Rover through the murky water, he said nothing, his jaw muscles popping in a steady rhythm, marking off the distance to the far shore. When the bridge workers cheered and waved as the vehicle crawled up the far bank, he simply lifted a hand and drove on. Only after we were out of sight did he climb out to hook up the fan belt again.

Then, at last, he became himself again. After he leapt back in, his face relaxed — "All right, men. The worst is behind us."

He drove on in high gear, whipping the steering wheel sideways to correct the Land Rover as it fishtailed in the mud left from yesterday's rain. The vehicle slipped and swung, but he corrected it expertly, swerving us back onto drier ground. Inside the cab my brother and I whooped. This was an amusement-park ride, Africa-style. The Laughing Hyena. Black Mamba. Crocodile.

We were only an hour from Soddo when the countryside began to look vaguely familiar. There was the sacrifice tree again, with the goat standing next to it, not yet gobbled up. Then came a long narrow puddle that Dad had skirted on the way out. With the rain of last night, the road had become one long pool, stretching out in front of us for thirty or forty yards. Dad could have driven into the grass and bypassed the whole thing, but he hardly hesitated as Johnathan and I begged him to drive through.

He accelerated into the puddle. The Land Rover slalomed from side to side, spraying a huge rooster's tail of dirty water. Johnathan and I yelled like cowboys on a bull. However, halfway down this long puddle, we were going much slower. And when we had gotten about two thirds of the way, we were hardly moving. This was not a puddle. It was a bog.

The Land Rover settled deeper and deeper, crawling along in slow motion, until the belly snagged and our wheels spun in one place. Dad lifted his foot off the gas. The screaming engine fell to an idle. After sitting back, he whacked the steering wheel. If his father could see him now, what would he think? A man worth his salt could take care of himself.

He rolled up his pants and stepped out of the vehicle. He stooped by each wheel. When he came back, his feet were clubs of mud. He didn't even bother to scrape them off on the running board. He just got in and started the engine. The Land Rover rocked as he shifted from forward to reverse, but it didn't lift out of its ruts.

Of course, Johnathan and I wanted to see for ourselves just how bad things looked — and of course Dad didn't want us to. But after awhile, he relented, so we piled out of the Land Rover and began clumping around, pulling our feet out of the quagmire in great exaggerated footsteps, like herons in a marsh.

While Johnathan tried to show moral support, I became fascinated by a foot-shaped puddle next to the road. I thought I had seen a little shadow shoot across it. When I looked closer, I found that I was right. I spotted a fat black tadpole, shaped like a teardrop. In fact, all the puddles were full of tadpoles, darting every which direction. When I put my hand into the water, it seethed.

I managed to scoop one of the tadpoles out of a puddle, catching it in a handful of water. I could feel its slick, froggy skin caressing my palm as it darted from one place to another. I pushed it with a finger, and it leapt right off my hand, splatting down into the mud.

When I looked up, I saw that the sun had sunk low over the distant forest. No one had passed by us this last hour, not even on foot. Suddenly anxiety washed over me like a cooling in the air. Being stranded at night in the open countryside in Ethiopia was not advisable. I knew that. There were still wild animals: hyenas, lions, maybe a leopard or two. And bandits were not unheard of.

"OK, boys, I need your help," Dad yelled. He began collecting rocks and sticks to lay down like tracks in front of the wheels. We jumped to this task, glad to be included. He even jacked up the Land Rover so that we could cram sticks and grass under each wheel. And somehow, miraculously, just as the sun was settling into the forest in a big brassy blaze, the vehicle bounded forward and screamed out of the mud.

Johnathan and I had been instructed to watch at a safe distance, so Dad stopped as soon as the Land Rover was on dry ground. He called for us to come, and we did, shouting with triumph. He turned off the engine, savoring this victory and shaking his head slowly.

For a moment we stood there with him, watching the sun as it blinked away in the far trees. I could spot some ghostly white birds circling over the forest, probably egrets. They opened and closed their wings like scissors, and I heard them calling out a high-pitched *cree, cree, cree.*

"Daddy, do you hear them?"

He listened for their far-off voices but shook his head.

"Do you hear them now?" Johnathan asked. "There they go again." But Dad shook his head once more.

He cupped his hands behind his ears and waited. And in the complete silence of the dusk, with Johnathan and me holding our breaths so as not to interfere, he finally smiled — "Like this? *Key? Key?*"

"Yeah, that's them!"

"You boys have such good ears," he said. "Good eyes too." He patted us on the backs, pulling us up to his sides. I could tell that he loved us, and I felt all alive as a result. I loved him too, even if he did get us in a mess sometimes. Dad took me places I would never have reached alone.

In My Father's House

DURING THE REMAINING WEEKS of Johnathan's rainy-season holiday, while we were still together as a family, Mom and Dad seemed to be making up for the weeks of separation. After the Land Rover adventure, Dad took us older boys hiking on Mount Damoto, where we accidentally stood in a colony of fire ants and had to strip to our underwear so we could pinch the flailing insects off our skin. On another day, we hiked to the stream below the mission, where we ate a picnic, enjoying the cool breeze that came off the burbling water as we splashed each other and flung pebbles at water spiders. Then one day Ato Wandaro came visiting, which prompted yet another family outing.

Wandaro was no ordinary visitor, like the lady who came selling eggs or the language teacher from the grade school who dropped by to practice English phrases, and that is why my parents always used the title *Ato* when they referred to him. He was one of the original ten converts who had survived persecution during World War II when the Italian army occupied the country and the Emperor was forced into exile. At that time, all the mission staff from the Sudan Interior Mission had fled Ethiopia, due to their connection with the Allied countries of England, Australia, Canada, and the United States. Because Ato Wandaro refused to recant his "English faith," the Italian soldiers (Catholics who considered him brainwashed) beat and kicked him, knocking teeth from his mouth. They tore clumps of hair from his scalp that never grew back, leaving shiny bald spots like pennies under his now-graying nap. However, he not only survived but continued professing his belief gently, kindly, even joyfully. When the missionaries came back to Soddo after the war, expecting to find their ten converts killed or backslidden, instead they found thousands who had been swept up in mass conversion and were asking to be baptized — all because of Wandaro and the faithful few who stood firm.

Dressed in a white wraparound *shamma* and canvas jodhpurs, Ato Wandaro tapped lightly at our screen door. As always, he carried a walking spear — a thin, oiled shaft of eucalyptus with a chisel-like iron tip and a knob of wrapped iron on the other end. He seemed to me like a character dropped out of a biblical illustration — one of the shepherds who had come to the stable in Bethlehem, or Elijah just back from his years in the desert fed by ravens.

As for Mother, her voice leapt an octave as she jogged to the door. She bowed respectfully, then held her right hand out the traditional Ethiopian way, gripping it at the wrist as if presenting it to Wandaro. She ushered him in and immediately offered tea and cookies. Then she sent Marta racing to the hospital to fetch Dad. Saint Peter might as well have dropped by, or the Apostle Paul. Indeed, when Ato Wandaro opened up his Bible, it seemed as if he had gotten it personally from God. He untied a chamois and gently lifted out the dark, worn book. He opened it with reverence, despite the fact that the pages were brown with the oil of long use and gave off a musky scent like animal hide.

Ato Wandaro wanted to know if my parents would come to visit a church far around Mount Damoto. There was little hesitation from Mom and Dad, who decided we would all go as a family.

That next Sunday, after we had been wrestled into our button-down shirts, slacks, and dress shoes, Johnathan and I bounded out the door with Nat close behind. We hopped our way down the eroded path to the stream, sidestepping muddy hoof prints and pungent cow pies, green as pureed spinach. We stopped for a pair of bent-over ladies with clay pots strapped on their backs, then made way for a man pushing a slipping donkey as it scrabbled up the muddy incline under a load of water tins. At the bottom, we leapt from rock to rock. Johnathan missed, and I liked the result so much that I missed too and stood for a moment, up to my knees, in the silty yellow water.

All the way up the other hillside, the two of us marched in step, enjoying the squelching sound in our leather shoes and Mom's raised eyebrow. Nat, barely a toddler, couldn't keep up, so he was taken captive on Dad's shoulders despite his loud protests. We climbed on into the hot, steamy air above the river ravine, then hiked another twenty minutes, arriving at last at the church Ato Wandaro wanted my parents to see.

Just like all the thatched *tukels* of the Wolaita people, this country church had a gray haystack appearance, but it was much larger — maybe forty feet across and twenty high. Mom and Dad stooped to enter, and the flies left their shoulders, alarmed by the change in light. I couldn't see after I stepped inside; I stood there blind and blinking. The air smelled sweet and ripe, like hay curing. I heard the murmur of voices in a buzzing chant. I supposed everyone was staring, and I felt defenseless against those stares; but in fact when my eyes had adjusted, I saw that most of the people were down on their knees, foreheads on the woven grass mats, praying.

Ato Wandaro got up from where he sat on a carved stool. He whispered to another man, who rose from his own stool. My parents lifted their hands in protest, but Wandaro pressed both stools on them. "*Gidelem,*" he murmured, meaning it was really no problem. They whispered, "*Betam ammasuganalow,*" and nodded appreciatively.

I felt awkward standing when everyone else was hunched over, so I plopped down on one of the mats as soon as Mom and Dad had taken their place against the thatched wall. Silently, I tilted my head back for a peek at the ceiling. Above me a series of hoops rose higher and higher, like the bands of straw in a woven basket, each one getting a little smaller than the last, until they closed around the massive center pole. I bumped Johnathan with an elbow and pointed up. He looked, then put his finger on his lips and lowered his head. I still gazed at the grassy dome, entranced by the pinpricks of light that pierced the thatch, sending down threads of whiteness. The only other light came from the doorway we had entered. The church felt wonderfully close and secret, like a cave.

A group of five singers took their place at the front, behind a roughhewn table. They sang out a line in Wolaita, to which the congregation replied. They sang out again, and the congregation replied once more. Johnathan had become very focused and sober. He mouthed the words of the refrain. I thought I recognized the song from the patients who chanted at night in the hospital. I tried to join in, but Nat leaned over and put his mouth against my ear, singing his own warm nonsense version of the song and nuzzling my neck. I pushed him away — "Cut it out."

"What are they saying?" Johnathan asked Mom eventually. She in turn asked Ato Wandaro, who had taken a seat on a log nearby. He whispered to a high school boy, who came and sat down next to my parents, his jacket and shorts giving off a sour wood-smoke scent.

This teen began to translate: "They are singing always the same thing. It means 'He is coming.' Jesus is coming."

The boy went on translating as a guest evangelist began his sermon. He whispered softly while the evangelist, an Amhara preacher, shouted in Amharic. Another translator stood next to the preacher, calling out each sentence in Wolaita as if trying to outdo what had been said. The three voices braided until they became a single rope of sound. I felt pleasantly close to all the listening people, yet distant. The blend of Amharic and Wolaita and English carried me into my own trance. My mind wandered back over the last few weeks, back to the white egrets circling over the forest and Dad cupping his ear to hear them, back to the water spiders skimming the stream as their tiny filament legs pressed silver dimples in the water, back to the bamboo corral and Madoqua's bristly brown spine.

The preacher suddenly ceased and everyone got down on their knees to pray, so I hunched over too, letting my forehead press against the woven mat, breathing in the sweet grass and the musky odor of earth. The voices around me, murmuring in Wolaita and Amharic, filled the cavelike room with mysterious desires and praise. I had my own thoughts and feelings. I tried to whisper a few — "Lord, thank you for water and birds and Mom and Dad and Johnathan and Nat." I felt a bit proud for trying to pray with no one asking, but I wondered if my English words had gotten through with all the others, or whether they had been lost in the general hubbub. Everyone else seemed so much more earnest and sure, as if they could see God standing right in front of them.

Later, Dad spoke to the congregation too — as another guest evangelist. "In the Gospel of John we read that Jesus is our bread," he said. Then he stopped for the interpreter to catch up.

"He is our water." Stop.

"He is the source of life." Stop.

"Only through Him do we have strength to do anything." Stop.

"He makes us *hylenya*." And here he turned to the interpreter, having switched languages. They conferred about what Dad meant by this Amharic word, *hylenya*. I knew what he meant. It was one of the words my parents used all the time in our house — to describe my brothers and me when we became coltishly active. It was meant to be a light, humorous comment, but the interpreter passed it on very soberly. I could tell that, for him, a sermon was serious business.

After Dad was done expounding on the opening verses of the Gospel of John, the original preacher stood up and asked if any wanted to become disciples this day, so that they could enjoy Jesus' life-giving strength, his "living water." Five people stood, and there was a murmur of affirmation. A wrinkled man stepped forward, followed by a gaunt-faced woman, then two girls about twelve years old and a tiny boy with knobby knees poking out of his gray smock.

The seekers left the room for counseling, and while they met with the evangelist and Dad, we sang some more and prayed. The service had already lasted for two hours, so Nat and I were growing fidgety. Mom had to hush me, so she leaned over with brownies she had brought in wax paper just for this situation. I nibbled on the chewy chocolate and became attentive again when the new converts came back. They had to share their testimonies, and their personal stories proved very intriguing. The teenager who was translating for us explained that the older man had been a thief. He whispered in English: "That man says he has tunneled into many, many homes. He does it at night, when people are sleeping. Then he takes things to sell, like bracelets or guns. He says he is sorry to do this."

The woman, another desperate case, confessed that she had had many "husbands." When the last one left her, her infant son had been bitten by a snake and died.

The tiny boy had panicked after leaving the church for counseling, dashing off into a banana grove. But the two girls were still here. They stared at the floor shyly, as they explained that they wanted to be changed — to feel different.

"God, help them each," Dad prayed, offering one last prayer: "Give them your bread of life, and your living water. Give them your strength to change. Let them find peace."

The Wolaitan translator turned this closing prayer into a Wolaitan prayer. We sang one last song, as a benediction. And finally we were done. Everyone stretched and rose. They all wanted to shake my father's hand before leaving. They all wanted to greet my mother. I was tired, but I was also quietly happy. It was not every day that I saw a thief and a bad woman and two girls, all wanting to know Jesus because of something my father had said.

On the way home that afternoon, after we had stayed for a feast of sourdough *injera* and spicy *wat* served in great heaps at the home of the minister, we slowly gained on a row of seven boys walking single file, poking at the rutted ground with sticks. Blind!

The smallest one had fallen behind. He called to the others, who were shuffling around a bend. They called back, and he left the path, striking out in a straight line. When he tripped and tumbled into a ditch, Dad jogged over to help him. Then one of the blind boys came back along the path, tip-tapping with his stick, cocking his head.

"The poor things," Mom said. "I wonder if we should lead them?"

"Please, not to worry," said the young translator, who had come along to escort us. "They do this many times. When they go to school for the blind."

"Our school? At the mission?"

"Yes, that one."

"What brave children," she said after we had passed the blind boys. "Can you imagine, Johnathan? Walking so far to school and doing it without eyes?"

"I bet I could do it," boasted Johnathan, and he picked up a stick, then closed his eyes.

"I can too," I yelled, and I grabbed a fallen branch.

Mom and Dad protested at first, apologizing to the translator for our thoughtlessness, but when he seemed unconcerned and they saw that we were out of earshot from the blind boys, they began to chuckle. Nat, who was riding on Dad's shoulders, laughed and laughed as we stumbled along, falling over sideways against the banks, bumping into each other, swinging our sticks like swords to make sure we weren't about to walk into eucalyptus trees — until eventually we both gave up and raced each other down the steep slope of the ravine to the waiting stream.

When they caught up with us there, then it was our turn to laugh because Dad had given Nat a stick and set him down. He slashed at the air madly, eyes closed. He shook his bleached hair as if saying a fierce *no* to our laughter. Then, dizzy from all his head-cranking, he lurched and tumbled on his back.

For that minute in the river ravine, we were all very happy to-gether — even Nat, who glowed after so successfully entertaining his older brothers. Mom and Dad, who were buoyed up by the church visit, seemed delighted that we could all be together in this experience, united in God's purpose. And for a moment, I felt the same pleasure. I sensed how we all fit together into something much larger than us.

My Brother's Keeper

A FEW DAYS LATER, we drove Johnathan to the airstrip outside of Soddo, and I watched with a strange mix of fascination and sadness as he climbed glumly up the plank into a DC-3, then roared away into the clouds with his pale face framed in the dark round window. Mom cried quietly and Dad squeezed her around the shoulders, and no one talked all the way to the mission station.

We shifted back into our routines. Dad disappeared after breakfast. Mom ran back and forth from our house to her next duty: hosting a sick Peace Corps volunteer who had come for treatment, teaching her health class for young women, preparing an English vocabulary test for the seventh-graders at the mission school. And I became the oldest son, saddled with a younger brother who couldn't keep up.

Marta, our housekeeper, had to take charge of Nat and me whenever Mom was busy, and she had a hands-off approach for the most part: she merely glanced over now and then as she cooked or wrung the wash. Every day, she wore a rough blue apron with her hair tied away under a matching turban. The turban was wrapped so tightly around her head that it felt like a ball of yarn. Sometimes, she would lean over and let me poke at the springy cloth. But on this particular hot, silent afternoon, she refused even that little entertainment. She had to finish hanging the laundry.

I felt sweaty and listless. Where was an older brother when you needed him? Even the *madoqua* had lost its appeal. After I climbed into its pen and knelt next to it with a hand on its back, the silent creature just nibbled at the grass, moving away in tiny increments until I was left alone. It looked as common as a goat.

"I wanna turn," whined Nat, who wandered up to the pen in his T-shirt, diaper, and red rubber boots. He shook the bamboo pickets and wailed until Marta came running and lifted him in. Then he tackled the *madoqua*, leaning on it so heavily that it panicked and backed out of his grip.

Bothered by Nat's clumsiness, I climbed out of the pen and ran for the other side of the house. There I found a little plot of roses in the backyard with a discarded tool lying next to them. Shaped like a small pickax, this tool had a hoelike blade on the front and two long prongs on the back. It gave me an idea. I could become a miner, or perhaps a pirate digging for treasure. I would dig in the moist black garden, picking through the straw and manure until I found something secret and special.

Marta holding Nat.

I hoisted the pronged hoe and thumped the metal head down. I needed more swing, so I planted my feet and lifted the tool higher. Marta must have lifted Nat out of the pen because I could hear him waddling up behind me. I dropped the blade onto the ground and turned.

"Go away. I'm busy."

He stayed there, grinning, so I pushed him on the chest and he plunked down heavily. His sun-bleached blond hair was almost white, and his face was flushed with the heat. He had recovered his customary cheerfulness — a kind of dogged happiness that made him smile even when I was being bossy.

After I had planted my feet again and begun to lift the tool, Nat hugged me around the waist. He mumbled, "I wanna turn."

"I'm warning you," I said.

I pushed him again and pivoted, lifting the hoe over my head, straining like a weightlifter. Back it went, the two sharp prongs flashing in the sun. But instead of swinging freely, it stopped short and bounced in my hands. I turned, and there stood Nat with eyes bulging. Before he could manage a scream, blood began seeping out of his yellow-white hair, dribbling onto one of his ears. I stared at it, paralyzed. I willed it to go back into his head and stay there, but it just kept coming.

Then came the scream: not outrage but pure pain, a high, involuntary shriek.

Marta flew from the lines of wet sheets and underwear, her blue apron flapping, her eyes wide in their sockets. She swept Nat up, murmuring the name of the Lord in Amharic — "*Gaeta, Gaeta, Gaeta.*" She swung her blue apron over his head and pressed it down. Then she ran with him.

I just stood there. Would he die? Had I killed my brother?

My face tingled as if I were short of oxygen. My legs were lead. This was certainly worse than anything I had done before, worse than bursting the glass Christmas bulb with my pop rifle or letting air out of the Land Rover tires or eating the yellow stem from the lily and getting sick. This had to be worse even than slamming Nat's fingers in my drawer when he tried to take one of my dinky cars.

I felt terribly alone and exposed, standing out there in the open yard with the hot breeze and the high clouds and the faraway ridge of Mount Damoto. Would my parents still want me? Should I climb into the avocado tree and not come down? When I finally found the strength to move, I instinctively raced to my bedroom and shut the door. Then I dove under my bed. Maybe I could hide there and no one would know — down with the dust balls and the broken toys, in limbo. I closed my eyes and prayed. I told the darkness I was sorry. And I waited for the judgment that must be coming.

Finally, Dad strode into the room. When he bowed to look under the bed, his face was flushed scarlet. His one good eye fixed me where I lay, holding me there like a nail. Then he dragged me into the open. But he didn't do what I expected. He didn't turn me over on his knee and spank me until my bottom turned into a raised welt. Instead, he marched me out of the house and down the road and right up the walkway into the hospital. And when we got there, he kept me moving through the patient ward, past the woman whose neck bulged with a goiter and past the red-eyed man shivering from malaria.

He pulled me right into the room where the nurses were shaving the top of Nat's head. He sat me down on a stool. "Watch," he said.

He went to work, and I did as told, watching as he lifted a syringe and needle out of the steaming autoclave to stick Nat in the head. I watched as he threaded a curved needle and hooked it through the edges of the torn skin, tugging as if he was trying to free a line from a fish. I watched as my little brother wailed and kicked and Marta held him down, unable to keep herself from moaning with sympathy. And when at last Dad lifted Nat off of the operating table — so that I could see my brother's face streaked by tears and dried blood — I felt I would never again lift a garden tool.

I had gotten in trouble before and been punished, but I had always nursed a sense of outrage. I had even thrown tantrums. This time I knew I was guilty. I felt the heaviness of my sin when I woke and saw Nat toddling down the hallway, his head wrapped in a ball of white gauze as impressive as Marta's blue turban. I felt guilty for weeks, even after the head wrap came off and Nat waddled around with a flat gauze bandage. Months later, when I would stand over him and look down into the little opening in his hair, I could see a slip of hairless skin the size of a paper clip, and I knew I was not innocent. Like Cain, I had struck my brother down.

Blessed Assurance

I WAS PROBABLY STILL THINKING about that slip of scarred skin weeks later when Dad suffered a gall bladder attack and had to be airlifted out of Soddo for emergency surgery. Death had always been a distant concept, something that restricted itself to the Ethiopian patients who came to our hospital. However, when we took Dad to the airport to be flown to Addis Ababa, he moaned like his patients. He didn't tell jokes as usual. While Mom and the mission pilot helped him into the little single-engine Cessna reserved for such flights, he seemed to be thinking hard about something he couldn't get out of his head.

Could a doctor die? I wondered. Could even my father die? And if he could, what about me? What would happen if I died? Would I go to heaven — or to the other place?

While Dad was away, Mom spent one afternoon assembling the figures and script for a flannelgraph program she would perform for the children's Bible club at Mrs. Barlow's house. With Nat napping and Marta gone for the rest of the day, the house seemed unnaturally quiet, almost spooky, as she pulled out the materials. A panel of black flannel served as the stage. Posterboard characters came in printed sheets, ready to punch out at the perforations. The characters had rough backings that stuck to the flannel board. They could be moved and dressed up and replaced as the story unfolded.

This week the story was about Shadrach, Meshach, and Abednego, the loyal Israelites who were forced into the burning furnace after refusing to bow to the Babylonian king. Since I was shadowing her, Mom let me punch out the three brave boys, who came as a unit linked at the hips. She put them on the flannelgraph board and dressed them in bright striped robes. I listened to her recite the story. Then she had me punch out the leaping yellow flames that she arranged around the Israelite boys — the great yellow-and-red tongues of fire that danced on the black flannel.

I wanted the straight scoop on hell. I'd heard about it before, but I wanted confirmation. Did it really have fires burning everywhere?

"This story isn't about hell," Mom replied. "It's just a furnace."

"I know. But is it true about hell? That dead people go there and burn?"

"You don't need to worry about that."

"Who goes there? Will the drunk man who got onto our Land Rover?"

As it had happened, just a few days before Dad's emergency airlift, we had all gone on a short road trip to visit a village church beyond Soddo, and on the way back we had been accosted by a man standing in the middle of the road with a rifle resting across his shoulders, his arms draped over the weapon. This unexpected would-be hitchhiker lurched to the window and asked for a ride. His eyes sagged and swam in their sockets. His kinky black hair looked scrambled on his head, and his breath smelled like curdled milk.

He climbed onto the running board and leaned into the cab to pinch my upper arm. He squeezed so hard the flesh throbbed. Then he leered at Mom and started to talk in a sluggish voice, not stopping except to wag his head as if clearing his ears of water. He talked and talked until eventually Dad had no other choice but to drive on slowly with the man hanging onto the window frame by one hand and clutching his rifle in the other.

I was greatly relieved when at last this unpleasant intruder *did* climb down, swinging his rifle back over his shoulders and staggering into the forest with his arms crooked over it. Mom and Dad explained that he was probably not always like this — that he had probably been drinking *arakea* or *tej*, the honey-wine that gave that lingering sick-sweet scent to the refreshment kiosk in Soddo. But their calm reassurances did little for me. I had never encountered an adult so out of sync with his own body. He represented a new kind of evil, something even worse than willful malice because malice was at least predictable.

This man's hard-to-forecast behavior brought him back to mind as Mom arranged paper flames around Shadrach, Meshach, and Abednego. She looked at me cautiously — as if she wasn't certain she wanted to go further on this conversation. She couldn't say for sure who would go to hell. That was between each person and God.

Then I asked what I really meant to ask: "What about me? Will I go to hell?"

I was remembering the garden tool and the blood on my brother's head, and though I felt afraid to hear her answer, I had to know. Maybe, since I had done something really bad, I wouldn't get into heaven at all. Maybe it was too late.

She became very careful about her words. "Timmy, no one goes to hell after asking Jesus for salvation. And children don't have to worry about that. Not until they're older. Not until they really understand."

"But what do I have to do?"

"When it comes time, just pray and ask Jesus into your heart."

"Did Johnathan already do that?"

"Yes, but . . ."

"Then I want to do it." I looked at her expectantly, standing up from my chair so that I would be at full attention.

"Right now?"

"Yes, Mama, 'cause I don't want to go to hell."

"Well, why don't we do it tonight before you go to bed. It's good to be really sure about a prayer like this. It's not like any other prayer, so let's just wait a little bit. But if you still want to pray tonight, we'll do that. OK?"

I couldn't understand the delay. This prayer seemed like a very urgent matter. What if I fell out of a tree today, like the boy with one leg, and what if I hit my head and died? What if I got sick like Dad and had to go to Addis Ababa for emergency surgery? Besides, wasn't this the whole point of my mother's work? Wasn't she putting together the flannelgraph so that boys like me would ask to be Christians?

I thought of the boys at her Bible club who had become Christians, and I thought of the people who had become Christians after Dad talked to them at the thatched church on the other side of the stream. How earnestly they had prayed, as if they could see God right in front of them listening. I wanted to see God that way — and to know I was one of the saved ones too.

I surprised her that night by bringing up the salvation prayer again as we got ready for bed. Nat had already fallen asleep in his crib when I whispered, "I'm ready to pray for Jesus to come."

She smiled at me gently.

"OK," she said, and at last she supplied the words I wanted. I repeated each one carefully: "Dear Jesus, I'm sorry for my sins. I want you to take them away and come live inside me." I kept the words in just the right order because I didn't want to slip up at all; it might mean the difference between heaven and hell. "I want you to come into my heart," I said, trying to be very precise about where Jesus could live. Then I concentrated inward on that heart-space between my ribs, anticipating the change that must be coming — the stretching of that pumping chamber, the movement as it accommodated the very presence of God. I was perplexed that nothing seemed to be changing inside, and I concentrated even harder, saying in my mind, *I really mean this. I want you to do it. Please?*

Finally, Mother broke in on my thoughts, saying, "That's terrific, Timmy." She kissed me on the cheek and hugged me tightly.

She smiled one of her big electric smiles, as if I had done something wonderful and way beyond my years. "That's the most important thing you can ever do. Your dad is going to be so happy. And Johnathan too. When we go up to Addis next week, you can tell them yourself."

I still felt a bit hesitant, not sure how different I was, but I thrilled at the thought of announcing what I had done. We would really be a family now. Not just Johnathan and Mom and Dad, but me too. And if Nat prayed soon, he would be saved. I would have to talk to him about that. Then we could all be together and stay together forever.

Come or Go?

AFTER DAD'S GALL BLADDER surgery, the incision became infected. He had to stay in the hospital on heavy doses of antibiotics, and it took so long for him to get well that finally the mission flew us up on another Cessna for a visit. He hugged me at arm's length.

Johnathan came to the hospital too — excited to get away from school for an afternoon — and when I announced that I had prayed to be saved, he threw an arm over my shoulder. Nat, who was always happy to get in on hugs, wrapped himself around my waist and wouldn't let go. Dad gave me a tentative hug, even lifting me a bit.

Then Dad let us look at his scar. He showed us the tilted grimace that ran down one side of his belly: an angry red where the skin puckered in. He stretched the gap and pointed to a missed stitch. Contamination had caused the initial infection, but now the silk in the stitches was causing a secondary inflammation. He went to work, dousing a pair of scissors with alcohol, snipping the stitch, tugging it free with tweezers.

A week later, when Dad had been released from the hospital, all of us but Johnathan flew back to Soddo on the Cessna. Dad was still cautious about lifting things, but he returned to work and Mom took up her support role. In the evenings after I had been put to bed, I listened to Nat's breathing as it settled. I never could fall asleep as quickly as he did. I heard the generator puttering to a stop and then the clicking of the Coleman lantern as Dad primed it. The mantle hissed after it was lit. That was the only sound, except a cricket keening from some hidden corner of my room.

Mom and Dad murmured to each other. She asked, "So what's the main thing you've learned these two years?"

"I suppose to keep slogging, even when I don't feel like it . . . And you?"

"That I'm not as good at this as I thought. I think I was more of a missionary in America."

Mom sighed, and I lay there thinking that I shouldn't be listening. This wasn't the way they talked around me. They wouldn't want me to think of them this way. However, I was too curious to block my ears. I slipped out of bed and tiptoed down the hall so that I could peek into the living room.

They were sitting at the dining room table under the hissing lantern, leaning together with plastic coffee cups in their hands. They seemed more intimate now than ever, due to the deep silence of the night and the pool of white lamplight. Fat yellow bugs circled the lantern, creating shadows that swooped and dived. The windows and doorways of our bungalow were black boxes opening on an impenetrable darkness.

Dad suddenly shook his head. "I shouldn't have sent that patient to Shashamane. They've got plenty of patients."

"But you weren't trained for intestinal surgeries."

"I wasn't trained for cataracts or bone grafts either. But who's going to do it? I figure I've got a hundred thousand people to cover. Dr. Barlow has a hundred thousand too. I mean there's no other doctor in the province. And the same thing is true at Shashamane. Maybe I just need to have more faith and try."

There was a pause, then Dad spoke again, wearily: "The thing is, Doctor Barlow actually likes the difficult cases. He'll experiment, if he has to. That's how he came up with the whole elephantiasis thing."

I was completely awake now and too curious to go back to bed.

I wanted to be included, so I made a strategic move and stepped into the lamplight, rubbing at my eyes.

Mom clucked. "Timothy Paul Bascom!"

"I can't sleep."

"Well, you can't sleep standing there. You get right back in bed."

"But what's that elephant thing?"

"Timothy!"

"I want to know about the elephant thing."

Dad smiled softly, pleased by my interest. He patted his thigh, so I shuffled over and sat on his lap. Then he started to explain: "It's not an elephant. It's a condition that makes people's skin look all hard or mossy, like an elephant's skin. You know those people who come to the hospital with fat legs — big as an elephant's legs? They've got the disease. Some people call it mossy foot."

"But how do they get it?" I wanted to know. He explained that some got it from tiny worms, but most got it because the soil had silica in it, which could penetrate bare feet like splinters of glass. If enough of those splinters got into a foot, they would overwhelm the lymph glands, which couldn't stop infections anymore. The foot would swell up to twice its size. It would stretch and crack and fester, and get as hard as bread Mom had overbaked — the bricklike stuff that she dropped out of the loaf pan.

"How do you fix it?"

Dad glanced at Mom, checking to see if he had clearance. She had cocked an eyebrow, but he decided to go on anyway. He told me that this sort of elephantiasis was almost impossible to cure. That nothing seemed to work. Except that Dr. Barlow was now trying something new that might be a solution: he would operate on the foot and peel the skin like removing a sock. Then he would take new skin from the person's thigh and put it onto the foot in a way that would make it grow.

"All right, young man," Mom said. "You know enough for one night." And Dad, taking the hint, picked me up and carried me back down the hall to my room.

He slid me under the cool sheets and rubbed my head to help me sleep. He might have left sooner, but I asked him a few sleepy questions — quick, whispered questions that led him to talk a bit more about his work. He explained how hard it was to operate on cataracts because of all those tiny stitches — especially since he had only one good eye and couldn't always tell how far apart things were. He whispered how satisfying it was to wire together a broken shoulder blade split by an ax in a brawl.

I asked him, "Daddy, tell me something difficult you did on children," and he told me about performing a tracheotomy and finding a bean stuck in a baby's windpipe. Then I felt too drowsy to quiz him, so I gave into the hypnotic motion of his fingers in my hair, scratching, circling, until I no longer knew he was there and he was free to return to Mom and the conversation I was too young to hear.

I turned five in April, and Johnathan came home three months later, having finished second grade. In September he went back to Bingham Academy for third grade. The rainy season gave way to the dry season, slowly transforming the fields and the valleys and the ridged hump of Mount Damoto from jade green to burned yellow. By the time Johnathan had come and gone again at Christmas, the farmers were out in the fields, bent at the waist, swinging sickles to harvest the *teff*. They carried the sheaves to the threshing floors, where boys walked beside oxen, spanking them in a tight circle around the threshing post, forcing them over the trampled stalks until all the tiny grains had broken loose. Wives and daughters winnowed the broken grain, scooping it up in woven trays, then tossing it skyward so the breeze would carry away the chaff in a cloud. Powdered with dust and flecks of straw, they all turned burned yellow, the color of the land. But Nat and I and Mom and Dad, we could never fully blend in. Even after three years in Ethiopia, every time we went somewhere outside the mission compound, children still chased us, calling out, "*Ferengi, ferengi, ferengi.*"

It was nearly time for our first mission term to end. In a few months we were due for furlough in the United States. Then what? Return for a second term or resume our abandoned life in Kansas? My parents didn't discuss the situation openly, although they sometimes touched on it during mealtime prayers or when we prayed before bed. They asked God to give us direction, to help prepare the way as we went home for furlough and considered the future. But mostly they just kept their thoughts to themselves and kept slogging. And on the days when they had no reserves left, they lay down. Naps had become important. Not just for us, but for them. They took them more often. On Sunday, always.

With only a few weeks left before we gathered Johnathan from school and departed for America on furlough, Marta asked if we could visit her village just once — to attend her church and meet her parents. Mom and Dad were busy with all the details of leave-taking: finishing the nurse-aide training at the hospital, packing dishes in barrels, hosting fellow missionaries one last time. However, they made sure that we got to Marta's village on the Sunday after she made her request.

We drove on a barely discernible set of ruts, skirting the base of Mount Damoto until we came upon a cluster of thatched houses with a tin-roofed church designated by a small white cross over its door. Marta was uncharacteristically absent during the service, leaving Mom to take care of us, and I could tell that Mom was getting frustrated when Nat and I squirmed so much that she had to cart us out to the Land Rover, now miserably hot.

If Marta had not disappeared, maybe Mom could have reentered the church and enjoyed the rest of the service. Instead she was forced to sit with us, cut off from everything and bored by our make-believe car racing. She grimaced as we wrestled for the steering wheel. When Marta did reappear, she asked in a stern voice what had kept her so long.

Marta explained that she had been helping her mother to prepare a meal for us. Then shame flashed across my mother's face like a spasm. She seemed to have lost her focus when we entered the house of Marta's parents. She looked around weakly, no doubt realizing the work that had gone into the thick stack of *injera* and the spicy *wats* set out in tin dishes. Then she began to comment on everything in sight. She told Marta how attractive and tasty the food was, not just the *injera* or the *doro wat* with its *beri-beri* broth, but the *alitcha wat* and the *zilzil tibs*. She commented on the main serving tray, with its red and green rim and golden Lion of Judah. She praised the rich flavor in the coffee that Marta's mother had ground and brewed. And when she noticed a set of smooth dippers hanging on the earthen wall, she praised them as well.

These dippers were made from gourds, but they were amazingly sleek and brown. "Aren't those lovely," Mom said to Dad. "They're almost like Revere Ware back in the States."

Marta had overheard. She passed this comment on to her mother, who got up and went to the wall and took down two of the polished ladles. She handed them to Mom, indicating that they were hers to keep. Mom shook her head, alarmed. She had not intended this at all, and it made her even more contrite, close to tears. However, she knew that she couldn't refuse now, for fear of offending her hosts. She took the gourds, trying to recover by saying a hearty thanks.

The generosity of Marta's family was heaped on our heads like coals that afternoon. After the meal there was a bag of roasted coffee beans for Dad, a cluster of bananas for Nat, and a live hen for me. I was afraid to hold the hen, even though its legs were tied. When we were ready to leave, we had to put it in the back of the Land Rover, where it stopped flapping and squatted nervously on a spare tire with one wing extended for balance.

Mom bowed toward Marta's parents before stepping onto the running board. She called out the window, "*Betam amusuganalow,*" which was Amharic for "thank you very much." Then she went completely silent. A few miles away from the village, she blurted out her first words, almost angrily: "It's not right. They have so little. They need that chicken. They need those bananas."

"Maybe they just enjoy giving," Dad said. "I think they really wanted to thank us for hiring Marta. At least we gave her an income."

"I know. It's just so humbling. I mean, we're the ones who are supposed to be the examples. But I feel like a dwarf. I'm a spiritual midget!"

Maybe that's the sort of thing my mother was thinking when she paused behind the house with Marta on the day we left Soddo for furlough. Johnathan had come home, having completed third grade. Our term was over. We were now giving up the house we had occupied and, with it, all the people we had come to know through the hospital and the churches of the Wolaita region. We were giving up Ato Wandaro and Markeena, and Marta too.

Mom and Marta stood in a strip of shade by our storage shed, where they had often gazed at the garden and talked about which vegetables to include with dinner. They were too far away for us to hear, but I saw Mom patting at her chest, which always meant she was sad. She came to the Land Rover crying. Hours later, on the flight out of Ethiopia, she was still heaving huge sighs, unable to answer our questions, just smiling a terrible, grieving smile.

Though I was worried for my mother, I was also excited to be on a jet plane — to be with my family going somewhere new. I didn't grieve about leaving Soddo because I didn't really think of it as permanent. This was just a trip; we would come back. I would return to the avocado tree and the *madoqua* and Mount Damoto. I would return to Marta too. Soddo was home after all. And the future was just some vague concept that my parents brought up when they prayed with us at bedtime. Since it was out of my control, I would leave it to them and God. Right now I was exactly where I wanted to be: thirty thousand feet above Egypt drinking Orange Fanta and snacking on a wedge of soft white cheese. I looked out the oval window, entranced by the blue sky and the white, white clouds.

Castaways

THAT SUMMER OF 1967, when Mom and Dad finally got us "home" to Kansas, they took us to see grandparents and to visit a series of supporting churches, displaying clay coffee pots, a horse-tail fly whisk, and a wide array of 8-by-10 black-and-white photos of Ethiopian scenes. Then they rented an echoing three-story house in Kansas City near the intersection of Southwest Trafficway and Thirty-first Street, and sat down to breathe.

Weeks gave way to months, and they still couldn't decide whether to return to Ethiopia — as though they didn't have the energy to think about it — so Dad took a job when one fell into his lap. An old family friend, the doctor who was caring for Grandmother Clara in Hiawatha, put Dad in touch with a doctor in Kansas City, who found him a local job at Bethany Hospital. He would be a "house doctor," filling in whenever and wherever needed, including the emergency ward.

Everything about our Kansas City existence seemed impermanent. When Johnathan tested into a gifted class, Mom and Dad had to enroll us at separate schools. I began first grade on my own, walking alone to Norman School, a fortresslike limestone building that was skirted on all sides by asphalt and had a high chainlink fence to keep balls from bouncing into the seething traffic. I took the five blocks at a fast clip, trying to look like I was sauntering when in fact I was on the panicked verge of sprinting. I quick-walked past the heavy-browed porches and the parked Chevrolets with their sharklike fins. I jogged from foot to foot while the crossing guard held me back at Southwest Trafficway. I knew to look both ways, but I wasn't concentrating on cars. I felt the vague dread of a six-year-old left in a busy adult space — the rabbitlike sense that I might become prey. I had seen fierce older boys chasing kids like me, sending them scurrying down sidewalks and alleys, and I was on constant alert.

Winter came and we still lived in this same improbable house in Kansas City, our lives still on hold while Mom and Dad listened for God's will. The house seemed like a kind of way station. Sounds echoed in the high-ceilinged rooms with their meager furnishings. No art hung on the walls, save a framed poster of an elegant table with gold place settings waiting on a sunset prairie. At the bottom of the poster, these cryptic words from Jesus: "Come, for all things are now ready."

When snow fell, I broke out of my daily speed-walk into a genuine gallop because now the older boys definitely chased anyone who looked smaller. More than once, they pelted me with hard-packed snowballs. I didn't like it here. I missed the hard-earned security of Soddo, with its deep-shadowed avocado tree and steady generator. I missed Marta, the kind maid with her blue bundled hair, humming tunes all day. I missed the place I considered home.

There was one haven, though. Once I had run the gauntlet of snowballs and barking dogs, and once Johnathan had arrived home on his yellow bus, I could play with him and Nat in the empty third story of our huge turn-of-the-century house. Up there, in that dimly lit, unheated space, we three boys would caterwaul and chase each other, safely removed from the anxieties of the street. Bundled in our winter coats, we climbed into the abandoned bathtub that stood on iron legs in the middle of the third floor. This became our pirate ship, and we sailed it away across the oaken ocean to the shores of an imagined Africa. Gray gusts of air billowed from our cold lips as we called out challenges. We fired Super-balls at the walls, as if fending off attacking frigates. No one could touch us.

Sometimes, if Dad didn't have to work the evening shift, he would entertain us at supper with stories about his patients at the hospital, like the crazy man he had to tackle and tranquilize. Or Mom would concoct one of her old bedtime stories about Sunny and Yum-Yum, the bunnies we had raised at Soddo. We would take "magic pills" and shrink so small that we could ride on the backs of the rabbits. We would go down into their warren, leaving the real world for a fantastic edible land of chocolate pleasure and not-too-scary adventure.

I had no idea as these months stretched into a full year that my mother and father were in the middle of a major crisis — that they weren't sure they had the strength or skills to return to Ethiopia as missionaries. I just knew that this house echoed and that we didn't have anything interesting on the walls, and I knew that we couldn't really stay. I felt out of place, like a foreign coin in a dime-store register.

Even the smallest activities were different from those in Soddo, so different that they had to be decoded like secret messages. We had no thatched churches to visit or egg ladies at the door wanting to barter. I would have found that sort of thing normal. Instead, we had to negotiate a battery of unexpected differences, like tiny grape-juice glasses for Communion, or the vacuum salesman wanting to demonstrate on our carpet, or the Mexican neighbor boys tempting us to tipple from the keg in their basement.

When truly significant events came up, they were all the more mystifying. One evening while Dad was still away at the hospital, Mom said something very important had happened and she needed to take us boys on a long walk. To our bewilderment, she said we would go as far as the World War I memorial near Crown Center. We knew that that memorial, with its carved obelisk, stood far beyond Southwest Trafficway, almost halfway to the skyscrapers of downtown, which made the unexpected journey seem extravagant and mysterious. It became even more remarkable the farther we walked, because other people joined us as if called out of their houses telepathically. Most of them were black, and so for the first time in a long while, I felt the weird familiarity of being a white foreigner — a *ferengi*. Yet it all seemed very different from anything I'd known before.

Mom's black friend Bessie showed up, and she and Mom linked their arms, looking very determined about holding onto each other. The others around us seemed sober and purposeful too, and though a few started to cry, they kept moving.

Finally, the crowd reached the lip of the hill where the memorial stood, engraved with its long list of war dead. There, everyone stopped and stood side by side, a little awkward now, as if they had just come out of a trance and were surprised at who else had joined the party. We gazed down at the austere, stone edifice of Union Station. We scanned the gray concrete valley and looked up the far hillside to the gray cityscape of downtown. Someone began to sing, and everyone joined in. It sounded like a hymn, but not one I recognized — "We shall overcome. We shall overcome . . ."

"Why are they singing?" I asked Mom.

"A very important man died today," Mom explained. "A minister and a great leader."

"Why did he die?"

But she had gone back to singing, and Nat was pulling at her other hand, wanting to be picked up.

"A man shot the minister," Johnathan whispered in my ear. "I heard about it in school. His name was Martin Luther King Jr."

"But why did they shoot him?"

"Shhh," Johnathan hissed, and he clamped a hand over my mouth. He looked around nervously. Then he leaned close and whispered, "The minister was black, but a white man shot him. That's because in America blacks and whites have lots of fights."

I looked around alarmed, with different eyes now. In Ethiopia, my white parents greeted black people with kisses. Even the men kissed the men. And afterward, they held hands as they talked. I didn't know that some whites wanted to shoot blacks.

Mom and Bessie were still linked at the elbows. Others were standing arm-in-arm too, but I could tell that touching was new for most of the crowd because they didn't look in each other's eyes or whisper like Mom and Bessie. They all stared straight out over the huge gray city, close together but lonely, singing with tears on their cheeks.

Life in America was baffling in ways like that, and sometimes frightening. So when at last Mom and Dad announced that we would be returning to Ethiopia, I clapped and danced. Soddo. Marta. Ato Wandaro. The one-legged boy. The avocado tree and Madoqua. Home.

PART TWO

Wave Goodbye

I HAD COME BACK to Ethiopia expecting to recover my hard-won home — to shift from a new and strange environment to what seemed old and familiar. Instead, the world I had yearned for did not materialize. Like my old pet chameleon with its whirling eyes, I wobbled and jerked on the palm of God. Yes, we had returned to Ethiopia, but I was not going to live at Soddo with my mother and father. This time I would stay at Bingham Academy with Johnathan. To make matters worse, Soddo wouldn't even be our station. The director of the mission had reassigned Dad to a barely functioning hospital near Leimo — a place I had never heard of before, where people spoke a completely different language called Hadiya.

"At Christmas, you'll see the new house," Mom said, trying to reassure me as we drove to Bingham Academy. "We'll go there first and get it ready. Then you can come."

"But why does Nat get to go with you?"

She picked her words carefully, gluing them together like pieces of a broken teacup: "It's not the same, Timmy. Look how little he is. Just think — you've grown up so much. You've already gone to school for a year. Now you'll get to be with kids your own age. Johnathan will be there too."

I remained dubious. As Dad swerved the Land Rover around

pits in the road and braked for donkeys, everything seemed familiar but wrong.

"Why can't I wait one more year? I could go to an Ethiopian school like the one at Soddo."

"Those schools are not the same, Timmy. You need to learn in your own language and be with American kids."

"But why can't you teach me? You taught kids at Soddo."

"Enough," Dad interjected. "We've talked about all of this. We wish we could keep you at home, but we can't."

So far Dad had stayed out of the conversation, clenching the steering wheel and avoiding the donkeys headed toward the Addis market with bundles of firewood or hay on their backs. Now that he had joined the fray, I looked to him for a hopeful sign. His jaw muscles were twitching. He might get angry if I pushed further. However, he might give in.

"If I can wait until Christmas, I won't complain at all. I promise."

Another cluster of donkeys trotted past. Behind them, barefoot farmers loped along with switches of eucalyptus, concentrating on the rumps of the animals the same way that Dad concentrated on the steering wheel. Stiff-faced, with wiry legs swinging inside their gaping shorts, these men didn't glance at us. Dad didn't glance at me either.

"Please . . ."

Mom sighed and adjusted Nat in her lap, where he slept while the wind from the half-open window swirled his white-blond hair. She looked away toward the blue mountains above Addis, stripped

DROP-OFF DAY AT
BINGHAM ACADEMY.
Johnathan and I stand at attention.

of their trees—away toward the green hidden hills of Soddo. She didn't look at me. Neither did Dad.

Finally I slumped back into the seat next to Johnathan. This was his role, not mine, I thought. After all, he was ten and I was only seven.

I peered at Johnathan but found no comfort there. Brows pinched, hair lifted in a startled poof, he stared out the window as if he knew he would be spanked as soon as the car stopped. I had seen him this way back when we took him to the airstrip at Soddo. I used to watch as he shuffled up the gangplank into the DC-3 for the hour-long flight to Bingham Academy, but back then I had been too excited by the drama of the event to fully absorb why he seemed sad. As the plane taxied down the grassy strip, preparing for takeoff, I relished the unfolding action. It disappeared over a little hill, then came tearing back at us full throttle. Mom sucked in her breath as the props ripped open the sky. Dad put an arm around her and pulled her to his side. The two of them gathered Nat and me, and held us in a tight cluster, hooked to the distant hum of that plane even after it had vanished into the clouds. The intensity of it all scared me, but I liked it too.

Today, though, I felt none of the old drama as we braked outside Bingham. The acrid scent of urine entered the Land Rover, carried to us from where an old man was leaning toward a mud wall. He glanced over his shoulder, unconcerned with the faltering stream between his legs. He tracked us with unfriendly eyes as we turned down the long tree-lined drive toward the school.

When we had reached the gate, my father honked the horn of our Land Rover, and the tin wings parted enough for a guard to step through, wearing his wool greatcoat. This *zebunya* saluted us and banged the tin with his cudgel, pushing one side open. He jogged across the road to whack back the other side. Then Dad took his foot off the clutch and we eased into the compound.

Immediately in front of us, the whitewashed main building, Gowan Hall, perched above a stone retaining wall. The brim of its tin roof was pulled down low over dark, unshuttered windows. On the red cinders of the parking lot, a cluster of kids in white T-shirts and jeans stood around a dusty tortoise. It paddled at the ground, straining its beaked head toward some far-off goal. Two boys lifted it by its black-and-yellow dome. They set it down pointed in the opposite direction, then glanced up as the Land Rover crunched to a stop.

I felt as if I were swallowing a malaria pill without water. A lozenge of panic lodged in my throat. What had seemed such an impossible idea a few days ago — just an abstract topic of conversation as we flew into Ethiopia — had now become hard reality. I lingered on the back seat. Dad had to open the door and tell me to climb down. Despite the novelty of the nearby tortoise, which spun slowly on its bowl of a belly, I felt no desire to enter my new world.

When I finally did step down, the cluster of kids around the tortoise stared at me. They saw Johnathan climbing out too. "Hey, Bascom," one of them shouted, and Johnathan lifted a hand noncommittally.

Mom and Dad had started walking around the sprawling administration building, so we ran after them. This hall was named "Gowan" in honor of the first Sudan Interior missionary to die in Africa — a fact that Johnathan had proudly recited to my parents back when we came to visit him. As the oldest building on the school grounds, Gowan Hall had evolved over time, growing outward from a smaller structure. Long, low dormitory halls radiated from the original two-story center, all made of whitewashed adobe and roofed with tin. To the side where we walked, a wide, tall dining room had been attached. It loomed over the narrow driveway, throwing down a strip of heavy shade. Here, the school fence, an eight-foot-high chain-link fence, was covered with sheets of leftover tin to keep passersby from gawking.

Above the brown-flecked metal, I glimpsed silver-and-green leaves, the tops of a young eucalyptus forest. I could hear disembodied Ethiopian voices. A boy, perhaps my own age, called out a strident curse — "*Yetabot!*" I recognized the snap of his whip, the tramp of hooves, the *cluck* that signaled he was herding cattle — probably helping his father take their humpbacked oxen to the river.

Back home at Soddo, I had a whip like that, with a smooth handle of acacia wood and a long strand of woven sisal. Dad had bought it for me from a local farmer. He had shown me how to spin it overhead, then snap it back in the opposite direction so that a wave traveled down the rope, jumping the tip with a loud *crack*. I wished I were at Soddo now, practicing that cracking sound as Dad and Tusuma loaded water tins at the stream. I wished I were standing in the delicious shade along the stream bed, where the hot air turned cool and damp; that I had a hand on the warm gray flank of the donkey, trying to calm it as the men balanced the five-gallon metal containers on the wooden carrying rack.

Instead, I was here in Addis Ababa, pinned down by a high-altitude, tropical sun that beat so hard on the galvanized roof of Gowan Hall that it made my eyes ache. Instead, it seemed that I might never return to Soddo.

The front doors of the building were wide open. All the windows had been lifted in their frames to let in the breeze. As Dad stepped into the shadowy interior to register Johnathan and me, a piano began marching stridently through "Chopsticks." Then a gang of kids yelled, so I turned toward that other sound, scanning the nearby soccer pitch.

Several children were backing away from another group, shielding themselves with the lids of garbage cans. As they retreated, they popped up from behind these metal shields and threw a salvo of eucalyptus acorns. Why were they crowing so victoriously, I wondered? Then I saw a boy in their midst, tied at the wrists — a black-haired boy like me, only two or three years older. He tripped, but they dragged him across the grass, staining his T-shirt. His face was streaked with dirt and tears. He looked up pleading.

The other children jerked this captive to his feet and hustled him into the tall woods at the far end of the pitch. A strange tightness constricted my chest. My hands hung cold. Though I followed

Mom to my dorm and listened to her greeting the woman in charge, Mrs. Johnson, I hardly noticed what was happening. Mom helped me unpack my suitcase. She showed me how to make my bed on the bottom of an iron bunk, pulling the stiff white sheet down tightly over the wool blanket so that the bed looked as hard and uninviting as all the others. I tugged at the sheet and the scratchy black wool, but I felt like I was not even in the same room — as if I were following instructions through the headset of a radio. The imagined chloroquine pill was back in my throat, undissolved and burning.

Everything was happening so quickly, so irreversibly. When we stepped out of the dorm, Dad and Johnathan were already waiting by the Land Rover, along with a half-dozen other families who had clustered around their own vehicles to murmur final, private words. Dad smiled wistfully.

"Got something for you."

He held out a red plastic yo-yo and demonstrated how it worked.

"You just flick it down, and when it reaches the bottom, lift your finger. It comes back up."

Johnathan pulled a bright blue yo-yo out of his pocket and tossed it down expertly, spooling it up to his hand. But when I tried, I couldn't raise the spinning plastic.

The dinner bell rang, and kids began to leave their parents, waving as they lined up on the cement steps into the dining hall.

"Well . . ." Dad muttered. "You shouldn't be late for your first supper. We better pray."

I saw him taking my right hand, and I saw Mom taking the other hand, but I couldn't feel their fingers. When they lowered their heads, I kept my eyes open, trying to see if this was all as real as it seemed. The rusty cinders mocked me underfoot. Although I saw them, I couldn't feel them pressing against the soles of my shoes. It was as if I were hovering in the air, reduced to nothing — a wisp of smoke, a scent breaking up on the breeze.

"Lord," Dad prayed, "you have promised to be with us in all circumstances and never to forsake us. Wherever two or three are gathered in your name, you are there. Please be with Timmy and Johnathan. Keep them safe, and give them strength and peace while we are apart. In Jesus' name, amen."

Johnathan added a few quiet words. I peeked and saw that his face was pinched in a tight knot, as if he could make things happen just by saying them hard enough: "Thank you, Jesus, for Mom and Dad and Nat, and help them to have a safe trip home. Help us to have a good time here, and help Tim to like it."

"Timmy, do you have anything you want to pray?" Mom asked. But I shook my head, realizing that nothing I said now was going to make a difference.

They hugged Johnathan and me, then kissed us on the cheeks, and with brittle, almost angry smiles they got into the Land Rover. Mom wrestled with Nat for a moment, trying to get him to look up. She blew a kiss. I thought to lift my hand to my own lips, but it wouldn't rise.

The Land Rover passed through the academy gates and receded between the walls of eucalyptus trees. Through the lifting dust, I could barely make out the shadows of my parents' heads. Then nothing. With a brusque crash, the *zebunya* slammed the tin gate shut, clanging the two halves together.

I felt as if I had tipped off a cliff and begun a long, long fall.

Cinders

DURING DINNER that first evening at Bingham Academy, I sat family-style with kids I didn't know, all of them different ages. The oldest, a tight-faced teenage girl, announced that she was going to be our table head. She told me I was at the wrong chair. "See that brown napkin ring? That's your place. From now on you always sit where you find your napkin ring. And no switching."

I shifted from the aluminum ring to the brown plastic ring, noticing that the table head had a carved ring with a cheetah on it. After she had led us in a long, stiff prayer I sat down like the rest. Then I stared at a bowl of mashed potatoes while she laid out her list of dining rules. Napkins in your laps. No elbows on the table. Don't speak while chewing. Eat everything.

"I won't let anyone leave until I see a clean plate," she concluded.

This was the cruelest rule of all, especially now, when every lump of food, no matter how long I chewed, stuck in my throat. The older kids spilled out of the dining hall first, eager to talk to friends or to use the last hour of sunlight for play. The younger ones, like me, sat around the half-empty tables chewing quietly and looking lost. I had been glancing over to my brother's table the whole meal, hoping to catch his eye. I forced myself to clean my plate just in time to shadow him out of the dining hall. I walked close behind as he shuffled toward his dorm, one of the long halls that had been added onto the original Gowan building.

Johnathan saw me following him. He glanced inside the dorm door, then jerked his hand, signaling for me to follow. "Usually you can't come in. Little kids aren't allowed. But it's OK since no one is around."

Two rows of metal bunks lined the side walls, pushed up against the whitewashed mud and straw. With the lights off and only dim twilight glimmering in the windows, Johnathan looked ghostly and insubstantial as he walked to his lower bunk. I began to cry. I sobbed so hard my shoulders ached. I felt like something big and monstrous was bursting out of me, like I might explode into a thousand wet pieces.

Alarmed, Johnathan put his arm over my shoulders and told me it was going to be OK. "Really. It only lasts for a while."

But I couldn't stop, so finally he said we should pray. We knelt down by his bunk bed with our elbows on the rough wool. "It's Satan that makes you want to cry like that. I used to cry just as hard," he explained. "You've got to deny Satan."

I was surprised. I had never thought of it that way. But since he had been through this before, I figured he knew better than I.

"Go away, Satan," I hissed in the gloom of the hall, with only the faint light of dusk in the windows. "Leave me alone."

"Say it in the name of Jesus," Johnathan explained. "Talk about his blood."

So I prayed again, "By the blood of Jesus, leave me alone."

I was spooked. I had never talked directly to Satan. It seemed dangerous to be challenging him. What if he got mad?

But Johnathan seemed satisfied. "That's right. Just keep praying like that when you feel bad."

He hugged me awkwardly, a foot taller. The way his kinky brown hair scrambled on his forehead gave him a thin, uncertain look.

"You'll be all right in a few days, I promise. It only hurts real bad the first week."

I nodded, trying to feel comforted.

"Well, you better get back to your dorm," he said. "You can get in trouble if you're not in by the bell."

I nodded glumly, then allowed him to put his arm over my shoulder once more and point me across the cinders of the parking lot.

"Just remember, God loves you," he said. Then he echoed what Dad said to us at night after prayers, saying the words awkwardly like he had to force them out of his mouth: "I love you and God loves you too." I shuffled across the cinders and up the ramp to my dorm. Then I walked quietly down the hard linoleum hall to my room, where six other boys were already assembled — six boys I'd never met before, six who had already been through this experience in first grade and knew how everything worked. I pulled on my flannel pajamas silently, greeting none of them. I followed them to the common restroom and brushed my teeth as they did, taking the boiled water from the white metal barrel strapped to the wall. I went down the hall to the living room of our dorm parents, the Johnsons, and sat silently through their welcoming comments and prayers. Several of the other boys gathered around to admire an empty tortoise shell that had been turned into a footstool with wooden legs, but I hung off to the side. Then I padded back to my room with these six PJ'd strangers, boys who would now sleep in the same room with me every night like my brothers used to do.

When Mrs. Johnson came to say good night that first night at Bingham, I closed my eyes so that she and all the strange boys would go away. She kissed me on the forehead anyway. She smelled like someone else's mother. When she flicked the light switch, I finally opened my eyes, feeling safer in the dark. I stared at her silhouette in the doorway — the wingtip glasses poking out from her temples, the unfamiliar flare of her skirt. She looked all wrong. Her voice wasn't bright and warm like I wanted it to be. Too matter-of-fact. How far away was my own mother? Was she still in Addis at the mission guesthouse? Or was she already at our new station in Leimo, scratching Nat's head as he fell asleep in his bed?

I waited, eyes open in the dark, as Mrs. Johnson stepped away down the hall to tuck in the other first- and second-graders. Her voice faded and went silent. The leaves of a eucalyptus rattled in the breeze outside our open window and glimmered ghostly white. Eventually I could hear the breathing of my roommates softening, but my own breath seemed louder than ever, and hotter. It seemed to whistle out of some pressure cooker in my chest, burning like steam. I willed it to stay down inside of me, afraid that if I let it erupt again, it would never stop. And I prayed once more, trying out one of John's new fighting prayers.

"Leave me alone, Satan. In the name of Jesus, leave me alone."

I found no strength in those words. If Mom and Dad and Nat were in a car crash or someone shot them, would I ever see them again? They could be dead right now as I lay there. So I prayed a longer, harder prayer, this time directing it to God like I was used to: "Lord, keep Mom and Dad safe, and Nat too. Don't let them have a crash or get hurt. Please, Lord. Please."

I prayed in silence. Even though I felt tears escape from my squeezed eyelids, no sound came up my throat. Dad had said Jesus heard us even if we just thought about things. He said God was with us in all circumstances. I hoped so, because I had no one else to talk to now.

Code of Conduct

SIX-THIRTY A.M. "Rise and shine!" Mrs. Johnson called down the cinder-block hall, trying to cheer us out of bed. We filed into the bathroom in our flannel pajamas, tiptoeing on the cold linoleum. We rubbed the grit out of our eyes while waiting our turns to pee and wash. The water was frigid. We splashed it on our faces anyway, blowing it off our lips, then trying to flatten our hair.

"Look at this," whispered the boy at the next sink. He pressed his strawlike hair against his forehead so I could see how it reached below his eyebrows, right to the middle of his nose. "By the end of this year, I'll touch it with my tongue. I bet I will."

This unexpected conspirator explained that we weren't allowed to have hair below our eyebrows. Since he had already been here for first grade, he knew what happened. He had seen it last year. If one of us got caught, Mrs. Johnson would send that boy to the Ethiopian barber who came on Saturdays, and that old man would rip around his head with electric shears until the hair was a uniform quarter-inch thick.

"Like a tennis ball," he said.

"Be sure to brush," Mrs. Johnson called as she poked her head in the bathroom door. He flicked his hair back coolly, acting as if we hadn't been having this conversation, and I took down the aluminum cup with my name penned on it. Other boys were going to the spigoted barrel strapped to the wall, so I followed them and got a shot of boiled drinking water. As I brushed my teeth, I examined the crooked line of my own bangs, which Mom had chopped back an inch before we left Kansas City for our return trip. How long would it take for my black bristles to grow as long as the other boy's? And what if my hair got so long I was caught? Would Mrs. Johnson write to tell my parents? Would Mom and Dad come to get me?

After we had dressed and made our beds, folding over the sheets so that each bed looked as wrinkle-free as the next, we boys stood around as though hypnotized. Then Mrs. Johnson called, "Verse group," and we filed toward the main door. Since we lived on the second story, we had to walk down a long cement ramp with metal handrails, much like a cattle chute. Several boys bolted as soon as they hit the ramp, but Mrs. Johnson shouted after them, "No running! Stay together."

The crisp morning air had a sharp, sappy scent from the wood smoke of cooking fires outside the school. Beyond the fence, the green-and-silver leaves of eucalyptus trees rattled in the breeze, reminding me of the forest in the valley below Soddo station, but I had no time to nurse homesickness. Mrs. Johnson kept us moving across the cinder parking lot to Gowan Hall, where the grade school girls were housed. Then she split us into smaller groups and pointed us to the rooms where we would meet our verse group leaders.

The first half-hour of each day was given over to memorizing scripture. As the youngest children at Bingham, my classmates and I were immediately assigned key verses such as John 3:16: "For God so loved the world, that He gave His only begotten Son, that whosoever believeth in Him should not perish, but have everlasting life." Or Romans 3:23: "For all have sinned, and fallen short of the glory of God." The woman in charge said that Solomon himself had recommended the best way to raise a child: "Train up a child in the way he should go, and when he is old, he will not depart from it," Proverbs 22:6. She explained that we had to learn six or seven verses a week, and that we each would get a gold star for every verse we recited correctly. If enough of these stars racked up on the verse chart next to the dining hall, then we could go to the Wabeshebele Hotel for lasagna or eat at the Addis airport and watch jets taking off.

I was interested in anything that might get me outside the fence of Bingham, so I went right to work, reciting each phrase exactly the way she said it. Then, at 7:30 sharp, she released us for breakfast, and we filed into the dining hall, joining all the other verse groups.

In the dining hall, the warped floorboards shone yellow under their varnish, and they creaked as we walked. On the walls stuffed birds hung, arrested in mid-flight, including a lilac-breasted roller with its azure wings spread and its scissor-tail snipping the air. There were antelope heads too, and the bulky striped head of a kudu with horns so massive and top-heavy that it looked as though it might smash down onto the table under it.

I hadn't let myself really look around the night before at my first Bingham meal. Now, as I waited for permission to sit, I scanned the room. I saw my brother Johnathan standing with some boys his own age, so I waved quickly with my hand in front of my chest. He didn't wave back, but he smiled a little, which made the day seem less scary.

One of the school administrators hushed us and opened with a long, this-is-the-beginning-of-something-large prayer. Afterward, I was careful to sit at the spot with the brown plastic napkin ring, as my table head had insisted the night before. I noticed now that the boy with the long straw-colored hair was sitting at my table too. He had a blue aluminum napkin ring.

"Everyone clean your plate," the table head reminded us. "No one leaves till the food's gone."

She spooned out a huge helping of oatmeal mush and passed it to me, giving me just as much as the teenage boy across the table. The mush was lumpy. The powdered milk was lumpy too, with little turds of undissolved powder floating in it. Only the sugar redeemed the stuff, and the table head threatened to slap us on the hand if we took more than a spoonful. Even so, while she was distracted by the kitchen help, the boy with the blond hair grinned at me and pinched some extra sugar out of the bowl.

When he and I had cleaned our bowls, we were excused, so we started toward the screen door together. He held out some of his contraband, which he had smuggled away in his closed fist. This sugar, unlike the refined white crystals we had bought at the grocery store in Kansas City, came in grainy speckled chunks that looked like rock candy. He offered me a few kernels and licked the rest out of his palm. I wasn't sure I should take stolen property, but it was too tempting. I cracked the little bits of sweetness between my teeth and grinned. "My name's Danny Coleman," he said, and I told him I was Tim.

We stepped out the door and descended the cement steps onto the cinders. I didn't know what to say, so I asked about a mattress that was hanging out the window of my brother's dorm. "How come they put it outside?"

"Oh, that's Morgan's. He's a bed wetter. He's in sixth grade but he does it every week. See all the yellow circles?"

"A sixth-grader?!" I looked at the mattress with incredulity. I was proud of myself; I didn't wet my bed. But I also felt secretly sad for the boy, whoever he was, to have this flag of failure hanging out his window.

I followed Danny because he seemed to know where we should go. For those of us in second grade, classes met farthest from the main building, clear across the soccer pitch and down a long sward of green grass to a two-story building where the unmarried teachers, all women, lived. Danny skipped in that direction, and I came along close behind. Cedar trees lined the fence down the hill, a screen against the prying eyes of Ethiopian children who might climb up from the stream and spy on our world. A few had made the climb anyway and were peering through, calling to us as we wandered down the grassy slope: "Hey you, my friend. Give me money."

Danny yelled back, *"Mininit lidgeoch?"* which was Amharic for "What kind of children?"

The children broke into gales of laughter and called out again, "One dollar, please." All the way down the slope they trailed us, clinging to the chain links with their fingers so they wouldn't slide down the bank into the stream. And all the way they repeated their request — "One dollar, please! Mister, one dollar," until finally we entered the classroom and their voices faded away.

The room was so dark after the bright tropical sun that for a moment I had to pause and blink. After my eyes had adjusted, I felt surprised to see, straight across from me on the wall, a black-and-white photo of Emperor Haile Selassie. It hung high above all the homemade educational posters with their blue construction-paper letters and red backgrounds. It was the same portrait that had hung in the waiting room at the Soddo hospital. Here was someone familiar at least, with his peppery hair and air force cap and hawklike nose. He had smiled at me when we went to the banquet at Soddo. He had waved me toward him in my dreams.

Our teacher told us her name — Miss Powell. She said she had just arrived in Ethiopia, but the way it came out made it seem like bad news. Her smile quivered. Her brows pinched. She lost track of what she had meant to say, and everyone looked sideways at each other. As the morning progressed, Miss Powell hesitated often and, during these lapses, boys began to kick each other under their desks.

By 10:30, when we heard the distant clanging of the school bell — a short length of train rail hanging outside the kitchen — Miss Powell looked both exhausted and relieved. She called out, "Walk!" but all the second grade boys sprinted from the room and up the hill, so I followed along, staying just in front of the girls. We ran across the soccer pitch and onto the asphalt road in front of Gowan Hall. We looped around the side of Gowan toward the dining hall, and there, on a concrete pad, card tables had been set out with platters of jellied toast.

I wolfed a piece down and headed back for another, but the Ethiopian kitchen worker stopped me. "One only. Play now."

Danny and some other boys were loping up the driveway to the soccer field, so I tagged along. For a while they raced around in a clump, attacking a soccer ball. When they wandered over to the pole-vaulting pit, I shadowed them again. The older boys had just quit vaulting, and I thought I might spot Johnathan, but he wasn't anywhere in sight.

Danny took over at the vaulting pit, lowering the wooden crossbar to a foot or two. I had no heart for it, so I just watched as classmates raced at the crossbar with bamboo poles. After a while, needing something to keep me from despondence, I picked up a pole and gave it a shot. To my surprise, I made it over.

"Great jump," Danny yelled.

He raised the crossbar and told me to try again. And again.

Danny was blond and exuberant, with elfin ears and a million freckles. I liked him. The others drifted away, but he and I stayed, still vaulting. In his imagination we were soaring above the heads of a great crowd, flopping onto the sawdust like Olympic stars. He clapped me on the shoulder and offered the highest praise: "Cool. You were practically flying." I began to believe I might even be what he saw in me — that I might be a happy victor, hoisting myself by my own strength.

A kitchen worker whacked the iron bar that served as our school bell, shattering this illusion. The children scattered, their voices whipped on the wind. I became aware of the wide-open field and how it stretched to each side. I saw the distant mountains, blue from the haze of cooking fires and diesel exhaust. I saw how high the African kites had risen, tiny black specks circling in the cloudless sky. Disoriented, I felt panic. Where am I? Who am I? How did I get here?

"C'mon," Danny yelled. "Recess is over." He began to run toward the towering eucalyptus tree at the corner of the fence, galloping around the bend and down the long green hill toward our classroom. I trotted behind, numb to everything around me. I recognized the whitewashed two-story building waiting at the bottom of the hill. Yes, that was my classroom, where we were going to practice capital letters after recess. But I felt no attachment to it or anything else in my surroundings. I ran toward the classroom as if it were something unbidden that had come to me in a dream and could not now be avoided.

During the next few days — even weeks — it always seemed strange to run down that hill toward the classroom. It didn't help that our first teacher, Miss Powell, got sick in the second week of school, or that after a number of substitutes our principal came to explain that Miss Powell wouldn't be back. When a replacement arrived, she was nothing like tentative Miss Powell. Miss Shepherd had been pulled straight from the Ogaden desert near Somalia. She had leathery skin and untamed shoulder-length gray hair. Just like the others, she had no husband or children.

The first day, she scolded me for staring at the ceiling: "You won't find any answers up there."

"Sit still," she commanded us all. "Do you realize how fortunate you are? I used to teach children who didn't have books. They didn't even have chairs. Some had to sit on the dirt floor. But they sat still!"

Miss Shepherd marched us through our printed alphabet, insisting that we start with the vertical descenders, not the horizontal slashes and loops. Each week she pushed us through writing letters to our parents at home. The letters began the same way: "Dear Parents, how are you? I am fine." After that she instructed us to capture on paper one or two things that had happened in the last week. I wanted to tell Mom and Dad how Danny and I had pole vaulted so high, but Miss Shepherd always seemed to have some other agenda, looking at me as if she might know better than I what my parents wanted to hear.

"What are you learning in verse group right now? Why don't you tell them about that?"

No matter how much I revised, following the dictated spelling that she barked out or erasing the reversed b's and d's, these reworked sentences seemed inadequate.

I wrote: "We are learning the books of the Bible in verse group." But what I really wanted to write was "Sometimes, even when I am playing, I get a strange feeling, like I have fallen in the middle of a lake and no one knows."

I wrote: "We heard that Miss Powell has typhoid. We must pray for her." But what I really wanted to write was "At night I wonder if you are still alive. Are you still there?"

I wrote: "I had only one mistake in spelling today." But what I really wanted to write was "I never get to talk to Johnathan. I miss the generator and the late-night baths with Nat. Please come get me."

Miss Shepherd patrolled the aisles collecting the wide-lined sheets of paper with their bulky penciled messages. "You need to finish up now," she announced.

I scowled at the traitorous words. I wanted to tear up the paper. Instead I wrote "Love, Tim." Then I let her take the thing away.

Three-thirty came at last. The kitchen worker whacked the iron rail. Another day at Bingham was half done.

Waiting Games

THOUGH DANNY AND I were different in temperament, the two of us had much in common. For instance, we were both good at remembering words. One Friday, we did so well on verse memorization that we tested out early and were allowed to play on the swings. As we competed to see who could go highest, Danny pointed at our classmates, still visible through a window in Gowan Hall, pausing as they forgot words.

"Those suckers will never get out," he chortled.

"I know," I said, and I grinned with satisfaction.

We pumped and stretched until the long chains on the swings went slack and we floated out of our seats, weightless above the soccer pitch and Gowan Hall, closer than ever to the dark, gliding kites that spiraled in the high blue. At the top of my arc, I could see beyond the tin-covered chain-link fence into the eucalyptus forest, where trails zigzagged away. I could see all the way to the bare green mountains. Bingham Academy had been built on the edge of Addis Ababa, right off a major road that led into those mountains. That road went toward Soddo, our old mission station. At least I thought so. But I had absolutely no idea in which direction the new station lay.

"Where do your parents live now?" Danny asked.

"It's a place called Leimo."

"I know, but where is it?"

"I'm not sure," I said.

He shook his head, as if he had no idea either. "My parents live in Obi. It's that way." He pointed away from the low morning sun. "We've got elephant grass so thick you need a hatchet."

I liked Danny because he said things like that. He insisted, for instance, that one time at his home he had swung all the way around the crossbar of a swing, loop-the-loop style. I wasn't sure if that was possible, but I wanted to believe him. I pumped hard myself. I wanted to do it too. Someday I was going to fly.

Danny and I played as if it were our calling, our own ordained mission. After school, we raced to the dorm to grab our matchbox cars, then raced into the eucalyptus forest, straight to the eroded bank near the communal garbage pit. We had been told to stay away from that area because the flies might carry diseases, but we always gravitated back because of a tilted strip of bare soil, perfect for playing with our toy cars, which we called "dinkies." The place smelled faintly of rotting vegetables and chicken entrails, but we liked being able to shape the ground. We dug into the bank and carved roads. We jammed sticks into the soft soil to form walls and roofs. We plastered them with sticky earth, creating whole towns of adobe houses with adobe roofs.

Roads wove between our miniature villages, Africa-style, without any grid; we drove the dinkies down those roads. I played mostly with my olive-colored Land Rover, the one Mom had helped me pick out before coming to school, changing gears with my voice and driving it over impossible terrain. I imagined the road to Bolosso, the one Johnathan and I had traveled with Dad two years ago when he took us on our epic trip and got stuck in the middle of the river. I imagined myself on a journey like that, going away with Dad and Mom to some new place where no one else had ever been.

Danny and I played with serious intent, as if it were a job. Inevitably, though, the time lagged. We became bored and wandered away from this clay bank, searching for something more fulfilling. We climbed trees and spied on older kids, or crept up on pigeons in the cedar trees and threw stones. One afternoon Danny suggested we sneak into the dormitory bathroom and take a tube of toothpaste that was nearly empty. Back to the garbage pit we raced, where we squeezed the pliable tube into a tight roll and took turns sucking the toothpaste. We bent and tore at the leaden tube until we had laid it open like a gutted fish. After we had licked it dry, we threw it into the garbage pit.

Finding food became a kind of covert mission. There were the extra snacks we could nab on Mondays at recess (when Sunday's pancakes had been rolled with jelly), and the not-yet-ripe peaches that we plucked from near the kitchen door (that is, when no kitchen worker was there to see us through the screen door and shout an Amharic version of "cease and desist" — "*Tow, unteh!*"). I even learned from Danny that the lining inside the bark of a eucalyptus tree could be scraped away like a sticky gelatin and licked from under my fingernails, so I stripped back the bark and nibbled at this stuff in little dirty clumps.

It was not that we were given too little to eat. We just always felt hungry — even after a large meal — and took pleasure as well in finding food that was off limits. One afternoon, Danny and I felt so bold that we did what we had only joked about before. We climbed into the locked pantry-shed by the kitchen, clambering over stacked boxes and squeezing through a gap in the eaves. Inside the dark, moldy room, after our eyes had adjusted to the strips of light thrown down through the slatted walls, we discovered a bin of potatoes.

"Lunchtime," Danny said, and he handed me two of the fattest potatoes.

"This is crazy," I replied, feeling a pleasant rush of adrenaline.

"Yeah, I know," Danny replied. Then he climbed back out and signaled with a soft whistle.

I tossed the potatoes to him and followed. Quickly, we ran to the trash incinerator behind our dorm and popped the spuds into the smoldering ashes. While they baked, we crept into the empty dining hall to "borrow" a saltshaker. One of the kitchen help saw us and came running, but the screen door slapped shut just in time, and he was forced to stop the chase. "*Yetabot,*" he cursed, just loud enough for us to hear as we scooted away, laughing.

For once we had more power than an adult. We knew that this man, as a hired Ethiopian, was bound to his workplace, so he couldn't risk chasing us. We skipped on the cinders before loping back to the incinerator, where the potatoes had blackened into fist-sized rocks. We broke them open and bit gingerly at the steamy pulp, shaking the salt right into one another's mouths. Then we hunted down some bulging snails on the concrete near a mossy downspout, and we poured the leftover salt into their shells, watching them writhe and melt. Afterward, we flipped them over and poured them out like snot.

I tried not to think about my parents and Nat during these long afternoons. If I was occupied, doing things with Danny, I didn't have to worry about them. They entered my thoughts only at the transition points, when I had to give up what I was concentrating on — like when the supper bell rang.

Then, suddenly, against my will, I became aware of myself as a solitary entity. My shadow stretched out thin and sticklike. Despite the promise of supper, I felt a strange emptiness. What was left to do with this day? What to focus on?

I imagined my father coming back from a day of work and getting down on all fours in the living room to tickle Nat, who would scream with delight. I pictured them both beside the orange cloth chairs with the zigzaggy arms, and Mount Damoto framed in the picture window . . . until I realized that this vision was all wrong. They weren't even in that house. They were not living at Soddo anymore. They were somewhere else, someplace I had never been.

During daydreams like this, when I accidentally began to reflect upon my situation, although I might be surrounded by the chatter of a hundred other children, time seemed to slow and grow heavy. After dinner I tried to enjoy the bit of sunshine left, but on the worst evenings I felt that I was not really playing. I was not really hitting the tetherball around the pole or leaping to stop it when my friend hit it back. And even if I tried to laugh, I was not laughing. I was waiting. Time was a weight pushing me under. True, this day was nearly done, but another would come like it, then another. All the same.

Candy Day

DANNY AND I HAD FASHIONED bows from the pliable green wands in a hedge, tying the tips together with string. We peeled thinner branches for arrows and went around hunting doves, careful not to pull back so far that the bows snapped. Always, the doves clapped away before our arrows reached them.

This was our game — a boy's game. Girls had their own games. They skipped rope, chanting weird poems. They made houses in the woods and furnished them with rocks and logs. Or they tended imaginary stews made of grass and leaves and acorns. We just tried to avoid them. We wouldn't speak to girls unless a teacher demanded it. And we certainly wouldn't touch them.

Inexplicably, one day when a few girls ran past giggling, I put out my foot and tripped one.

I think I felt as shocked as she did. This girl had a sweet, dimpled face. She had seemed pleasantly removed from the world until brought back so rudely. She hugged her scraped knee, pressing her fingertips around the raw flesh. She looked up with tears caught on her eyelashes. Why had I done this?

I had no answer. And though I felt I should say sorry, I didn't because Danny and another boy were right there watching.

"You better get out of here, in case she tells," they whispered. So I walked away, feeling as if some alien force had taken over my limbs momentarily.

Aside from that strange contact, I avoided girls altogether until one afternoon when Danny and I were hunting doves in the cedar trees behind our dorm. We spotted two girls from our class holed away under a canopy of branches, and Danny had a surprising idea: "Let's ask them to be girlfriends."

"No way. Everyone will tease us."

"Not if it's a secret." Once again, Danny had introduced something unexpected and dramatic. He always seemed to have new ideas. Tired of being the follower, I pretended to resist, but I soon relented because I liked the prospect of doing something daring.

We ran back to the dorm and wrote notes. After we had attached these to our arrows with rubber bands, we crept back to where the girls sat under the cedars, then leapt up and shot our bows. My arrow waffled into the branches above their heads, and they glanced up. We waited just long enough to see one of them open the note. It said simply, "Come to the cave."

The "cave" at Bingham was a tunnel dug by some of the high school boys in the clay soil at the farthest end of the soccer pitch. There, the flat ground broke away and sloped into the forest, sheering off at a chain-link fence and plummeting to the silty yellow stream. A round hole, like the open mouth of a fifty-gallon barrel, opened into the hillside. Danny and I had been inside partway, but we had spent only a minute there, chattering to scare away whatever bogey-monster might be lurking further in. As a result, I still didn't feel like I had ever really seen this cave.

We drifted around the playing field, eyeing a group of boys who were playing soccer. When no one was paying attention, we scrambled down the slope, slipping on the bare ground. The excited calls of the soccer players faded high in the silver leaf canopy. We could hear the stream burbling below us and the sharp laughter of Ethiopian women slapping river rocks with their wet laundry. We bowed cautiously and peered into the entrance of the cave. We half-expected an older boy to lunge out. However, after a moment's hesitation, Danny whispered, "C'mon, there's nobody in there."

Cool air seemed to be exhaled from the cave as we crawled in. I shivered and paused, waiting for my eyes to adjust. Whoever had dug the cavern had hacked it out as if cutting wood. The chop marks of the spade could be seen like a series of broken dinner plates. I reached out to touch a wall, feeling the moist clay, cool and smooth to the touch. I plucked a root tendril and breathed in the pale-yellow mushroom scent. I could not hear the soccer players anymore, only the faint peal of laughter from the washing women, and the whine of a mosquito.

Danny was deeper into the tunnel, back where it split in two directions and circled around a column of earth. "Check this out," he murmured, pointing at dozens of shadowy letters carved in the clay: J.B. + R.D., B.A. LOVES S.P., ESTHER I LUV U.

A mosquito stung me, and I slapped it, losing enthusiasm. I thought about the eighteen-inch rule that the teenagers complained about — the one that stipulated all boys must keep eighteen inches of space between them and their girlfriends. I wondered what would happen if we got caught down here with two girls. What were we going to do with them anyway?

I had very little experience with girls, so I had reason to be nervous. While Danny had two sisters, I had none. Only one girl my age had visited the Soddo compound during my toddler years. While our parents talked, she and I had tried awkwardly to play together in the backyard. We crawled inside the tent Dad had put up to air. She wanted to play house, but I didn't know how. I asked her.

"Let's lay down together and hold each other tight, because that's what my parents do."

"OK," I said, and I wrestled with her, rolling and tugging, not sure whether I should try to pin her to the ground. My legs intertwined with hers and something huge hummed inside of me, something bigger than all the little bells of excitement that came when I touched myself in bed at night. Everything seemed erased except the warm, waxy scent of that canvas tent and her body. I felt the pliable warmth of her thighs and stomach, the same temperature as my own flesh. I didn't want to move. I lay completely still, swallowed up in awe. When at last she got up and went out of the tent, I stayed. In part I simply wanted to extend this deep bliss — like floating half-asleep on an inflated raft when the breeze is just cool enough to be refreshing. But part of me stayed inside the tent for a different reason: I was afraid that someone would see and know and wonder about such a small boy having such a big experience. It was like God himself had talked, and I wasn't sure that I should have been listening.

"Maybe they aren't going to come," Danny said from the gray shadows at the back of the cave.

"Yeah, I guess not," I replied.

But then we heard thin voices, and the cave mouth turned dark. Mary and Janet had climbed down the embankment to peer in.

The girls' dirty knees poked out from under the hems of their skirts as they kneeled and smiled at us. We stared back, then crawled out solemnly, blinking in the bright sunlight.

"All right," Danny said. "I think we should sit in a circle."

He arranged us on the ground just outside the cave mouth, with dark-haired Mary next to me and blond Janet, who was short like Danny, seated next to him. Then he led us in an odd transaction.

"We want you to be our girlfriends, OK? If you agree, then you have to promise."

They nodded, but he wasn't satisfied. "You have to promise out loud. And we do too."

We took turns pledging ourselves to one another. At first I wasn't sure which girl was to be mine, but since Danny pledged to Janet, I figured I should pledge to Mary.

"Mary, I promise to be your boyfriend," I said, risking a quick look at her dark curls and freckled cheeks, and glancing curiously at her cat's-eye glasses with the little rhinestones glinting at the corners.

"I promise too," she said, smiling in a way that made me wonder whether she meant it. She seemed to be appraising me, as if my price had been fixed too high.

I glanced to the crown of the hill. What if one of the other boys in my class was spying on us at this very moment and about to shout: "Hey, check it out. Look what Tim and Danny are doing."

I wanted to go, but Danny demanded one last promise: "Every candy day, we have to trade candy. OK?"

The girls nodded and grinned. On Saturdays we got a little cache of candy from our parents to savor throughout the week, and trading was standard practice. However, no second grade boys ever traded with girls, so this was a daring and intriguing idea.

"But where are we going to meet?" asked one of the girls.

"Under the pine trees by our classroom. Nobody goes there."

"OK," said the girls. They giggled, then leapt to their feet and ran away. Danny and I raced the opposite direction, swooping between trees like doves flushed from cover.

By Saturday, when I lined up with the other boys outside the candy closet, I think I had half-forgotten our deal with the girls. Mrs. Johnson lifted the tins one at a time, calling us forward to dole out rations. Mom had packed my candy in a green Christmas tin with slender Currier and Ives skaters gliding on a silver pond. I was sure it came from Kansas — that other world where not so long ago I had lived in a three-story chilly house and walked to school past older boys with snowballs, the same world that had made me want to come back to Ethiopia where I supposedly belonged.

Mrs. Johnson held my tin firmly in her hands. She wouldn't let any of us hold the tins for fear we would spill the contents. I felt her impatience and began to choose candies as quickly as I could. First, a Mars bar. Then a roll of Life Savers.

"Life Savers count for three days," she said. "So now you're down to three smaller candies. That's the rule."

I picked two butterscotches and a peppermint, and she closed the lid.

When I turned away, a friend named Steven jumped at me, wanting to trade a stick of licorice for a peppermint. I was about to agree, but Danny grabbed me by the elbow and shook his head: "Don't forget. The pine trees!"

I was surprised we were following through with our plan, so

I trailed Danny nervously across the school grounds to the long, green slope that descended to our classroom. I half-hoped the girls had chickened out, but when I saw them waiting under the pine trees, I felt a secret delight. They were sitting cross-legged with all their candies spread out on their skirts. We plunked down beside them, forming a circle, none of us sure what to say or do. However, once we started to unwrap the candy and to trade, touching sticky fingers, we all grinned. I spontaneously hung on to Mary's hand while I savored the thick sweetness of a caramel she had swapped for two Life Savers. Danny and Janet were holding hands too, smiling broadly.

We weren't supposed to eat more than one piece of candy a day, but what did we care! We ate them all in one sustained rush, enjoying our sugary feast. Mary and I risked actually looking at each other for a while, as we rolled the Life Savers in our mouths. She squeezed my hand a little, seeming shy about it, not really like the almost-sassy girl she could be. It scared me. I remembered now what Danny had told me: "You know, if you hold a girl's hand long enough, she might have a baby." I wondered how that worked and whether we should stop touching each other for a minute. Just then I spied our teacher, Miss Shepherd, stepping down from her apartment above our classroom.

From fifty yards away, Miss Shepherd seemed very alone as she concentrated on the steps, her frayed gray hair hanging to each side of her face and turning it into a hidden grotto. She straightened at the bottom of the stairs and swung toward us. We all froze. Up the hill she came, walking on the path that would pass by only a few yards away. We watched silently, trying not to betray ourselves by the slightest movement or sound. However, she stooped instinctively when she had drawn near. She peered under the low-hanging branches, spying us where we sat in our little circle, hands still clasped.

I expected her to growl or to race at us. After all, we were breaking the eighteen-inch rule, and we were only seven-year-olds. Instead, a soft, almost sad, smile came over Miss Shepherd's stern features. She straightened up, so that her face was hidden behind a spray of pine needles, and stood there a moment, completely silent, before starting up the hill again toward the soccer pitch and Gowan Hall. She moved in plodding silence, mysteriously merciful.

"Oh, man, we better get out of here," Danny exclaimed, and we all scrambled to our feet. We left the candy wrappers where they dropped, running single file between the row of pines and the chain-link fence until we reached the top of the hill and had to break from cover, scattering in four directions. I was oddly elated but nervous. Would Miss Shepherd turn us in? Would Mary get pregnant now that I had held her hand so long?

I wasn't sure, but in a way I didn't care. I was glad that I had a girlfriend. I hoped we would meet again and trade candy next Saturday. I wanted to hold her hand and see that soft, small smile that didn't have any judgment in it. I wanted her to look at me like she saw who I was and really cared.

Moon Landing

CHRISTMAS VACATION NEARED at last, and I allowed myself to think of my parents and my younger brother. Five days and we would be together again. Four days. Three. Then, at last, the morning of departure arrived and instead of experiencing pure bliss, I woke divided, torn between anticipation and calm indifference.

After breakfast I hung out on the cinder parking lot, eyeing the tin gates as the *ʒebunya* opened them. First came a VW van, then a white Peugeot station wagon greeted by a shriek of recognition. Next came a flatbed truck with welding tanks lashed in the back, but no one ran to meet it because it was driven by our dorm father, Mr. Johnson.

When would they come, I wondered. And why was I almost afraid for them to appear?

Dozens of other children had congregated near the entrance, chasing each other across the cinders, skipping rope, punching a tetherball. My brother Johnathan was there too, throwing acorns at a rust spot on the fence. However, when Danny came running, I let him convince me to wander into the woods. He was acting as if this was any other day, so I tried to do the same.

At my core, I knew that this *wasn't* any other day, which meant that my anxiety kept swelling like a bottled scream. While I rumbled my dinky Land Rover down a hand-carved road, I felt an internal pressure so strong that it threatened to spurt out. Itchy with worry, I couldn't play at playing. Had something happened to my parents? Had they changed plans? Were they leaving the school right now with Johnathan in the back seat, having given up on me?

"I gotta go," I blurted out.

"Naw, just a minute."

"No, my parents might be here. I gotta go."

I raced through the eucalyptus forest, past the other kids on the rickety merry-go-round and past the shed where Danny and I had stolen potatoes. I sprinted along the latticelike walls of the gymnasium, until I was on the edge of the cinder parking lot. Then I braked and stood behind a line of wet sheets put out by the laundry women. I scanned the area, trying to calm my breath, to not look too eager. What would they look like? How would they act? For that matter, how would *I* act?

I saw all the other kids still yelling and running about. Then a horn blared from beyond the gates. The *ʒebunya* rose out of his plywood booth, shoving back one section of tin. A green Land Rover, covered with dust, eased into the school compound. And, yes, it was them.

My knees went weak, as if I had stood up for the first time after a long illness. I stepped from behind the drying sheets and strolled toward the Land Rover, smiling shyly, my hands in my pockets. I didn't want to rush whatever was going to happen. But Mom threw open her door and spread her arms wide, so I let go of my tough-guy act and ran right into her embrace.

Johnathan arrived a second later, so she grabbed him too. Then Dad wrapped us all in his arms and Nat got down on his hands and knees so that he could burrow his way to the center, grinning to reveal his missing teeth. Holding onto them and marveling at the solidness of their waists and arms and legs, Johnathan and I started to bubble over with a stream of words. We were checking for responses, wanting to make sure they were still who we thought they were. We talked about classrooms and friends and pole vaulting and candy and whatever else came to mind.

Danny showed up as they stowed our bags in the back compartment, and they wanted to know who he was, so I introduced him. Then he stepped back, looking more sober than usual. As I climbed into the Land Rover, I felt sorry that he had to wait longer than me, but I was too happy to worry for long. The terrible gates had swung open. We were driving out — out into Addis Ababa and beyond. I was with my family again.

At that moment, I think I believed I could go anywhere, as long as we went together. I knew that we would not be returning to the familiar, old station where we had lived before going on furlough. I knew that Marta the maid wouldn't be there to greet me. I would not wake and go to the window that looked out at the humped back of Mount Damoto lined with brassy sunlight. But I didn't care. The paradoxical beauty of being so cut off from my parents and little brother was that now I could feel exquisitely connected. The emotion felt sleek inside me, and elegantly fragile, like blown glass.

After we had cleared the edge of Addis Ababa, the road changed from pavement to gravel. Bouncing in the back seat, my brothers and I whooped at each pothole. The gravel gave way to dirt, and the road began to dip in and out of ravines, crossing rusty dry-season streamlets. Anyone else on the road was walking or trotting along on a donkey or mule. We drove instead, carrying extra gas in jerry cans so we would have enough to make it all the way to the new station. When one of the tires went flat, punctured by a three-inch-long acacia thorn, Dad took the spare off the front grill and bolted it on. "Pray that does it. It's the only extra." Then on we rolled, away from Bingham and Addis toward the place I had never been, the place Mom and Dad called home.

My parents might have been to this new station before, but for me our journey was taking us into uncharted territory, so it was not hard to imagine us as a group of intrepid explorers going where no person had gone before: into the heart of the world's largest desert, or down into the shipwreck depths of the ocean, or out into space like a character from the Tom Swift novels that Johnathan liked to read, the ones with titles like *Tom Swift and His Space Solatron* or *Tom Swift in the Race to the Moon*.

As the hours passed, though, reality took over from my imagination. I grew sore from the swaying and jolting. A haze of dust whirled through the cab. My brothers and I had nothing to amuse us now except the occasional anthill that towered up six, eight, ten feet above the baked ground. We had reached the semi-arid wasteland that we used to drive through from Soddo to Addis, and we were following the edge of it, turned dumb by the flat, grassless landscape and the thin layer of acacia leaves lifted up high over the plain.

Far out in front of the Land Rover, a dark figure rose out of the heat waves and wavered there. As we drew closer, I realized it was a tall girl with skin that shone like oil. She stood on the roadside watching, with a bundle of sticks balanced on her head. She had no shirt, and her new breasts, the size of small oranges, stood out proudly. Mom asked to stop. She wanted to take a picture. However, when the girl saw the camera, she laughed and turned away, still balancing the sticks. She wore a skirt of bark strands and a necklace of cowry shells, studded with bright red and blue beads. She couldn't speak Amharic, and Mom and Dad didn't know any words in her language, so it was a stalemate. We drove on, leaving her in the middle of the road with her back to us, bowed under the weight. The only living creature in miles.

A few more hours of this cracked, unrelieved brownness, and then the road climbed a bit. The flat plain began to ripple. Eucalyptus trees appeared in the low places. Toiling under the late afternoon sun, bare-chested farmers tugged weeds from their fields of *teff*, a milletlike grain that stood yellowing in the fields, almost ready to harvest. We followed a thin stream for five or ten miles, and arrived at last, removed to a world quite unlike my boarding school in Addis Ababa and a hundred times further away from the three-story clapboard house we had occupied in Kansas City.

. . .

Compared to Soddo station, Leimo was far less established. Soddo had been around since pioneer missionaries pitched their tents in 1927, but Leimo station had not been opened until the fifties, then stood empty for a few years as the mission searched for replacement staff. Wheel ruts broke off from the main road and disappeared into the shallow stream, petering out as we topped the far bank. A low hospital stretched out in front of us, looking antiseptic with its whitewashed walls and tin roof. And behind it, fifty yards apart, stood three stucco houses, like a town that hadn't taken hold.

The wonderful thing about these boxy little houses was that they were painted bright, unexpected colors — aqua and lilac and lemon yellow. Though they seemed delicate and out of place, they gave Leimo station a cheerfully eccentric air, like a carnival in the middle of nowhere. Ethiopian homes, by contrast, seemed nondescript: round instead of square, earthen instead of painted, thatched instead of tin-roofed. In the Leimo region, in fact, many of the houses did not have true walls. They were entirely grass-covered, looking more like haystacks than houses. Now, at the height of the dry season, they had literally disappeared into the countryside, indistinguishable from the sunburned fields.

Johnathan and I hooted as we ran into our lilac-colored home, dashing through the smooth-walled rooms, which were actually mud and wattle under their whitewashed exterior. This house fit us well — clean and solid and full of cool air. It would be our oasis, our safe place.

We learned soon that seven other *ferengis* lived at this station, since they all came rushing to greet us. There was a single nurse who came quick-walking from the hospital, and a family of six called the Dyes, who spilled out of their house and ran to the Land Rover. One of the Dye girls, Mary, was in fact my girlfriend from Bingham Academy. As it turned out, her parents had just been re-assigned to Leimo, like my parents. So it was just the twelve of us (and one more nurse who arrived a few weeks later) plunked down together in a remote valley in southern Ethiopia to form our own tiny community.

Several days later, on Christmas Eve, the Dye children came over and congregated with us in our kitchen to make holiday taffy. We took turns buttering the warm blobs of candy and stretching them into ribbons. Mary and I got on opposite ends of one handful and pulled it so far to each side of the kitchen that it hung like a long strap between us. We ate mouthfuls of the salty stuff while it was still soft and wonderfully chewy.

Night came quickly — at six-thirty — and after we had waved good night to the Dyes, we stood on the porch and gazed up at a sliver of moon, bright as platinum. Aside from the Dyes's flashlight, not a light could be seen in any direction. The river valley stretched out silent and black before us. The ridges of the valley were visible only as a darker blackness than the sky, where thousands of stars blinked and sparkled, white like the incandescent particles that fly from an arc welder.

As we boys put on PJs and climbed into our beds, Mom and Dad lowered a precious Christmas album onto the portable battery-powered phonograph, and Bing Crosby crooned out his baritone version of "Silent Night."

"Sleep in heavenly peeeeeace," he sang, letting his smooth voice slide through the vowels, flowing into our candlelit room like warm syrup. Then, suddenly, on the other side of the window above my bed, a loud cackling broke out as if a gang of maniacs were amused by the music.

Johnathan and I lurched in our beds.

"What was that?" I whispered.

"Just hyenas," our little brother replied, speaking up proudly.

"Right in our yard?" I asked.

Dad had stepped into the room. "Don't worry, hyenas are showoffs. They stay up on the ridge. Now you guys go to sleep. You want to get up for presents, don't you?"

I *did* want to get up for presents, but I also couldn't shake the hyenas out of my mind. It was a long time before I slept. Then suddenly morning had arrived, pale in the windowpanes, and I heard a scratchy sound in the living room, broken by occasional squeaks and whirrs. Mom's best-behavior voice spoke a string of carefully enunciated numbers and words: "9, echo, echo, 52. This is Leimo checking in. Do you read?"

A pause, then a scratchy voice from two hundred miles away: "Roger, we read you. Merry Christmas. Hope all is well. Any traffic today?"

A pause, then Mom's voice, again strangely clipped: "All's well. No news to report. Over and out."

"Roger that. Over and out." Then silence.

No news to report? What would there be to report? Immediately, I sensed the tenuousness of this radio contact, which would continue to wake me every morning that first holiday, reminding me that we were dangling on a lifeline in unmapped territory, far from the world we belonged to. We needed to be checked on, just in case.

I was too excited by the proximity of Christmas to ponder the situation for long. The hyenas were gone, daylight was in the windows, the scent of cinnamon and chocolate hung in the air. I called out to my brothers, "I dibs the first present." Then I raced for the living room.

One of the few disappointments of Christmas Eve had been the announcement that we would not have a Christmas tree. Mom and Dad had explained that the people from this area, the Hadiya, were not accustomed to missionary behavior, so they might think we worshiped the tree. To our delight, when my brothers and I sprinted into the living room, we found our parents grinning beside a spindly eucalyptus tree adorned with strings of popcorn and paper ornaments. We hooted, and Mom and Dad glanced out the living room window, worried that our celebration might draw attention. They were determined not to let any nationals get a glimpse of us in "pagan revelry." However, their caution made Christmas only more exciting because now it was clandestine. I tore into a package wrapped in brown shelving paper and found inside a set of eight new matchbox vehicles, including a fire truck with a ladder that actually swiveled and extended. Nat got a trike. Johnathan got a box kite. And from Uncle Paul in Seattle came a Tupperware container full of Kool-Aid, hot cocoa mix, Three Musketeers bars, and other American delicacies.

Judging from the Ethiopian kids who congregated around us when we emerged from the house with this loot, the only toys available locally were the whirligigs made by bending and pinning together eucalyptus leaves like a propeller, or perhaps a handmade car with a wire body and bottle-cap wheels. We boys, by contrast, had just been supplied from the great treasure chest of the West.

Johnathan built his box kite quickly and asked to take it on a test run. Nat was too little to keep up, but Dad allowed me to come along with them. I got several turns, running down the windless valley, dragging the resistant flying machine. Johnathan tried to shout it aloft — "Pull, pull, pull. It's going up, I think it's going to fly" — as if enthusiasm alone could make the thing soar. It rose to twenty or thirty feet, as long as we kept dragging it. However, after two miles of this, we had to surrender because we were blocked by a small gorge. The box of balsa and red paper settled limply to the earth and Dad, huffing, caught up with us. He and Johnathan shared mutual frustration. I, on the other hand, felt good just to have gotten so close to succeeding. In fact, as long as we had kept running, the kite *had* stayed in the air. As far as I was concerned, it *had* flown.

We stood a moment on the lip of the little canyon, trying to get our wind back. A gang of children had followed us down the valley, fascinated by our experiment in aerodynamics. They had grown in number the farther we went. Now fifteen of them surrounded us, staring at Johnathan and me, many of them older and taller than either of us. Each of the boys stood with his weight on one leg, shepherd-style, resting the other foot against the locked knee. They leaned on their walking sticks and began to whisper secret messages in Hadiya, a language that I had not yet heard. It sounded similar to Amharic, but I couldn't pick out any word. Finally, the biggest one dared to direct his voice at Johnathan.

"You. Whaddis your name?"

Johnathan ignored them. I did too. We rankled when Dad began to talk to them in Amharic, tossing in occasional Hadiya words and gestures as he tried to cobble together a conversation. We resented the intrusion on what could otherwise be focused time with our father — the father we had not seen for over two months. He had taken this day off from the hospital. This was our first real chance to be alone with him, and instead we were being interrupted by complete strangers.

The Ethiopian children whisked flies from their faces and stared, as if they expected us to do something entertaining. One squatted to peer at Dad's leather boots. They all giggled when Johnathan put his hands in his pockets. We turned to head home, and they scattered, screeching. Then, after gathering their composure, they circled back. They dashed in front of Johnathan and me, staring into our faces in hopes of a reaction. They threw questions at us in their mother tongue and called to the oldest boy, who tried to translate.

"Thaddis what?" the tough boy asked Johnathan, extending his chin toward the kite. When Johnathan didn't answer, the boy poked him in the arm — "You, my friend. Thaddis what?"

"A kite," Johnathan spat out angrily, and all of the kids scattered laughing. "Uhkite," they said to each other, trying out the new term they had learned. "Uhkite. Uhkite."

I looked at Dad for reassurance, a bit intimidated by the number of them, seven or eight on each side, loping along in packs. I felt hemmed in and misunderstood. These boys lived in clay-and-grass lairs. The whites of their eyes were filmy and red, irritated by wood smoke and mold and the dust that fell from the slowly deteriorating thatch. They had virtually nothing metal in their homes, except the steel blade of their father's sickle or machete. No matchbox cars. No Bing Crosby on the phonograph. Not even a can of sardines.

I felt completely removed from them, and it didn't help that they spoke this new language. At Soddo I had been able to join in on conversations now and then, learning words from Marta and our gardener, then trying them out on the children who walked by from the mission school. Here, though, I was forced to start over again on their terms.

"*Ttuma*," the boys called out. It was a greeting, Dad explained. But the way they said it — like an explosion in the front of their mouth — sounded like a challenge. And when I tried to say it back, they laughed. I didn't talk to them anymore.

There were so many reminders during that first holiday at Leimo that this was not my old home at Soddo — odd little incidents that impressed me with a new sense of vulnerability. Such was the night that my brothers and I got into a tickle war with Dad. When he blew out the candle, we leapt on him in an ambush. He tossed us on our beds and tickled till we laughed more shrilly than the hyenas outside. Then Johnathan fell to the floor, and when he got up, he writhed and screamed. He did a crazy dance, clawing at his legs, his back, his hair.

Ants!

A whole colony of driver ants had marched into the room under the cover of night and were streaming toward the hallway. When Mom came running with another candle, we could see the glistening trail of insects, and we followed it to where they were invading the house under the kitchen door. Because Johnathan had dropped across their trail, they had gone into attack mode. Now Mom swept and Dad sprayed, and we couldn't sleep for another hour, until all the tiny black carcasses had been removed and eucalyptus branches had been laid down around the perimeter of our room.

"It's OK now," Mom said. "They don't like the oil in the eucalyptus, so they'll stay out."

"How do you know?"

"Because Mrs. Schmidt told me, back when we lived at Soddo."

I was comforted but not fully convinced. We were at risk out here, and I knew it. Yet I also felt oddly happy. At Bingham, though I had been ensconced in a walled fortress, surrounded by Addis and its daily reminders of the Western world, I had been numb much of the time. Here, at Leimo, I was an interloper, but I felt much more alive.

After the ants had been dispersed and I had slid back into the warmth of my covers, I sat a while looking out the bedroom window at the high white moon and at the sharp black shadows that it threw down under the orange tree and the clotheslines. I loved just sitting there, hearing the calm breathing of my brothers in the beds next to me and the occasional grunt of my father in the next room. I felt cut off from the safe, predictable world I had known in Addis, but I had my family to compensate. Our shared foreignness, like the sweet comfort of being under a tin roof during rain, gave me a strong sense of security. The danger was out there beyond the window, in the dark, and that made me more sheltered here, inside, with my brothers and my parents.

It would not happen for another seven months or so, but in my mind one last incident is linked to that first Christmas holiday at Leimo. After Johnathan and I had gone away to school and come back again in July 1969, Johnathan began to talk about something entirely unimaginable: "Did you know a man is going to walk on the moon?"

I was old enough to know when I might get duped. This sounded like something out of one of his Tom Swift novels, so I shook my head in disbelief.

He smiled a very superior smile. "Uh-huh. It's true. You can ask Mom."

I ran to the kitchen. "Mom, Johnathan's lying. He said a man's going to the moon."

"Actually, it *is* true. God willing, in a few weeks some American astronauts are going there on a rocket."

Was it possible? Could Americans actually do that? People like me?

The night of the scheduled moonwalk, July 21, my parents woke us at four-thirty in the morning. We sat with them in the dark, listening to the BBC radio broadcast on a short-wave radio, like the one we used daily to check in with the mission headquarters in Addis Ababa.

Set on World Band instead of Private Band, this bulky radio brought in the distant announcer, speaking solemnly and authoritatively about the expense behind the Apollo space flights: "The sheer cost of this program, of course, continues to be a matter of controversy. Thirty billion dollars for the Apollo program. An American I was talking to last night remarked that, for that much money, they should discover God."

When we heard this sacrilegious comment, Johnathan and I looked over at Dad, expecting a reaction, but he was too engrossed to respond, so we concentrated again as the announcer explained that Neil Armstrong and Edwin "Buzz" Aldrin were perched in their tiny craft on the Sea of Tranquility, chosen for its smooth landing surface, and that Armstrong was donning his space suit in preparation to leave the capsule. I looked out the living room window, where moonlight etched the top of our climbing tree with silver highlights. We had just finished building a tree house, and the rope of the tire swing dangled below, silhouetted against the silver grass.

Then Armstrong was out of the ship, taking the rungs one at a time. After a pause, his calm voice scratched into the room, staticky with two hundred thousand miles of space dust, sounding not unlike the voice we boys woke to each morning as Mother tuned into mission headquarters in Addis.

"One small step for man, one giant leap for mankind," Armstrong proclaimed. Then, after a pause, he made his first, matter-of-fact observations about the ground under his feet: "The surface is fine and powdery. It adheres like powdered charcoal to the sides of my boots. I only go in an inch or a fraction of an inch, but I can see my footprint."

On the hillside above our station, hyenas were cackling and hiccupping, bigheaded and mangy. Out there our Ethiopian neighbors were asleep on the clay floors of their thatched houses, next to the dying embers of night fires. Their hens, which had been brought inside for safety, were clucking nervously from roosts against the walls, lifting their sleepy heads into the smoky air, blinking, settling back into sleep. But all the way around the globe, where the night was still young, people were celebrating in the glass-and-chrome NASA headquarters, eyes on their dials and electronic monitors. They were tuning in, like us, as President Nixon came onto the broadcast to congratulate the astronauts: "Hello, Neil and Buzz. I'm talking to you by telephone from the Oval Room at the White House, and this certainly has to be the most historic telephone call ever made . . . For every American, this has to be the proudest day of our lives, and for people all over the world, I am sure, they, too, join with Americans in recognizing what an immense feat this is. Because of what you have done, the heavens have become a part of man's world."

Ethiopia was still asleep under the moonlight in houses that had not changed since the time of Jesus, while out there on a fragile lifeline of communication, two men were tiptoeing across ground that had never been touched by humans. Two Americans were out there in the deep distance — hooked up to the same source that provided my family with box kites and taffy, Christmas albums and Kool-Aid. They were stopping to stare at their own impossible footprints, the first human prints stamped in the thick dust of the moon, permanent as a sculpture, not to be disturbed by wind or rain.

Johnathan and I were uncontainable. We ran out on the porch of the house with Nat, cheering so loudly that Mom had to hush us, afraid we would wake the Dyes. A new day was just beginning to lighten the eastern horizon, but the sky to the west was an almost-black blue, and we looked up in awe at the white sphere floating there.

"I think I can see the 'nastronauts," Nat said.

"Really?" Mom replied. "Where?"

"Just in the shiny area, where there's a black spot."

Johnathan and I grinned at each other knowingly.

"Wake up," I said. "Nobody can see that far. Not even God."

"Uh-hummm," Dad warned.

"Well, maybe God, but not Nat."

"I can too," insisted Nat.

"Can not."

"Can too."

"Enough," Dad interjected, and we boys finally desisted. We stared up at that incredibly crisp wafer of light, feeling very far from it and somehow connected too. It seemed so surreal and dreamlike, in part because we were usually asleep at this hour. In Houston it was 9:00 P.M. on July 20, but here in Ethiopia it was 6:00 A.M. on the next day. Even time was different.

I tried to imagine — under the clean light of that moon — what Armstrong and Buzz Aldrin might be feeling as they looked back at Earth. And for a moment I thought I might have a glimmer of understanding. I sensed that, in some way, what they felt might not be that different from what I felt while looking up toward them. Distance. And a remarkable sense of being set apart, utterly removed.

My World, Their World

NO TRUE ROAD came to the Leimo station, only the rutted drive-way crossing the stream or the dirt paths that local people used for walking and herding. The main road, the one that came from Addis, lay on the other side of the valley, and it bent toward Ho-sanna, a small town fifteen minutes west by automobile, thirty by mule. This road was so invisible in the bunch grass that when a lone truck or bus growled past it seemed to be plowing through open savannah.

We lived on the east slope of the valley, and we were always looking west, across the narrow stream and its attendant trees. Over there, beyond the strip of bottom land where the Addis road passed, we could see an uncluttered rise with maybe three or four thatched houses, each one surrounded by thorn fences and banana trees. We would watch a farmer moving across the fields, sickle in hand, crouching and cutting the *teff*— step-swoop, step-swoop. Or we might see a boy running out of a thatched house in pursuit of a hen. But it all happened in silence, at a distance. By comparison to Soddo with its bustling school and its large hospital, Leimo was a quiet station in a very quiet valley.

The days grew longer. After the initial excitement of escaping school, Johnathan and I, who were accustomed to a daily schedule of activities, found ourselves fidgety. We lay around complaining that there was nothing to do. Nat echoed us, although he sometimes turned to the Dyes's youngest children, Cathy and Mark, as alternative playmates.

Johnathan and I weren't as comfortable initiating play with the Dyes's older girls, especially in front of each other. We wanted something else to do, and for a while we tried climbing the drop-offs by the stream, using the sisal rope Dad had bought at the Hosanna market. Johnathan would anchor the rope around his waist and toss it over the clay bank. Then I, lighter than he, would shinny down ten feet, until I could touch the murky water. When he hoisted me back up the vertical wall, I twisted and kicked and sent planks of clay slapping into the water. Never mind that the stream was only a foot or two deep, or that I was climbing only two or three times my height; I still imagined all sorts of incredible crises. I was a deep-sea diver on a cable, a polar explorer in a crevasse, an astronaut suspended in space.

Eventually, though, we wearied of this ritual and fell to complaining again. Johnathan, who was always planning something big, had been begging Dad for one special favor ever since we arrived at Leimo — a horse. Now he brought it up more often, and I supported him, knowing that I too might benefit. Finally, halfway through our first Christmas holiday at the new station, Dad agreed that if Johnathan would do extra household chores he could have a horse.

So Gillian, the speckled gelding, came to live in our yard, spending most of his time grazing in front of the porch, flanks twitching, tail whisking, as he stretched to the end of his tether rope. We rode him bareback: no saddle, just reins. Then we rode him on a western saddle that Dad found in a storage barrel left by former missionaries.

Actually, most of the time only Johnathan rode Gillian, while Nat and I simply watched. When Johnathan allowed me a turn, I walked the horse or took a short trot. Cantering would have been smoother, but the speed of a canter was too much for me to bear. The flexing and shifting of all that muscle, the drumming of the hooves and the blur of wind — all gave me a sense of something too large, too powerful to be safely controlled.

Instead of asking to ride alone, I sometimes just climbed on behind Johnathan and held him around the waist. We covered a lot of terrain that way. We followed cattle trails the length of the valley, going below the waterfall to a rugged area where the horse had to scramble through gullies or weave through stands of eucalyptus. We squeezed our legs tight and ducked as Gillian sidestepped and lunged. Then we crossed the stream and headed back on the other side of the valley.

It was there that we came upon the flat, grassless strip of land that served as an emergency landing strip for the mission's Cessna. Although the landing strip lay unused almost every day of the year, it had to be smoothed regularly. Recently, Dad and Mr. Dye had tied a log behind the Land Rover and dragged it back and forth, uprooting woody shrubs and tearing the tufted grass out of the ground. When we looked down that narrow field, so wonderfully flat, we realized it was a perfect place for racing a horse.

Johnathan let me down and kicked Gillian into a run, one arm out to the side so that he could slap the horse's rump. I shouted encouragement. Then my yells attracted a local boy who was trotting his horse in the opposite direction on the road to Hosanna. When he saw these *ferengis* testing their horse's speed, he turned down the slope to offer a challenge. He and Johnathan conferred at the far end of the landing strip, using hand signals and gestures. They lined up side by side, paused a moment, then kicked their horses' ribs, bouncing high as the horses strained toward a gallop.

Both of them leaned low as their steeds stretched into a full-out canter. They clutched the horses' manes, letting the animals take over, hungry to run. As they thundered toward me, they seemed to be moving so fast that they would not be able to stop. I ran behind a thorn tree and watched. Gillian won by a length, but Johnathan had a hard time bringing him to a stop, calling out "Whoa" and leaning back on the reins until finally the horse stood still, breathing heavily.

Once Johnathan had turned Gillian and started him toward me, my brother lifted his head to thank his competitor. Because he knew no Hadiya, he called out in Amharic, *"Betam amusug-analow."* It was evident that he wanted to talk with this boy, unlike the ones who had been shadowing us for weeks as we climbed the stream banks or wandered on the cattle trails. However, the other boy turned away on his horse without acknowledging the friendly gesture.

"Ttuma," Johnathan called out, using the only Hadiya word that he and I knew — the word of greeting. But the boy just lifted his head in a proud nod and kicked the horse's ribs, trotting up over the shoulder of the road.

"Hey," I said, "don't worry. You beat him fair and square." But Johnathan didn't join me in the celebration. He watched the path where the boy had disappeared, and when I asked if he would run Gillian again, he seemed to have lost interest.

"He's run enough," he said. "You know it can be bad to run a horse too much."

Back at the house that afternoon, Johnathan didn't want to play, and I was content, for a while, to do something alone. I liked to draw, so I pulled out an old *National Geographic* and tried to sketch a giraffe from one of the pictures. I enjoyed the concentration — the way time slipped by as I focused on the wobbly legs, the curving neck, the random spots. I knew that Mom and Dad and my brothers were close and available, so I rested in this quiet activity, coming back to it after dinner and focusing closely on the lines, not distracted or anxious.

The next morning I spent more time on the drawing — that is, until Dad came back from staff devotions at the hospital and sat down for a quick pre-work coffee break. Mom, energized by having everyone under one roof, fired off several conversation starters. She wanted Johnathan and me to know how much work had been done to improve the Leimo station: "You boys need to realize nothing looks like it did three months ago. When we came, the house wasn't painted. Do you remember, Natty?"

"Mom's right," Nat said. "It was all dirty and stuff."

"There was no garden. The grass was up to Nat's waist. And the patient wards were a complete wreck. We had to chase birds out of one wing. Your Dad even did his first operation on a door that had been laid across two sawhorses."

"Really?" Johnathan asked.

Dad, slow to speak in the morning, nodded his affirmation.

"So wasn't there anyone here before you and Dad came with Nat?"

"Actually, there was one person," Mom said, and she exchanged a quick glance with Dad, whose face had tightened.

"Who?" I asked.

"Nurse Marie was here for a whole year, all by herself. She couldn't run the hospital, but she saw patients in the clinic and gave them medicine."

Mom looked to Dad again, who seemed to have found something that tasted bad in his coffee. I was intrigued, but a knock at the front door called Dad away before I could gather any further clues.

Four Hadiya men stood on the porch to see him. The spokesman for this small group was a stern, close-cropped man dressed in canvas shorts and a shawl. He kept pointing toward the hospital with his horsetail fly whisk, then toward the floor of our porch. The others nodded, murmuring their assent and looking at Dad suspiciously.

"What was all that about?" Mom asked after Dad came back in.

His jaw muscles rippled. "Their relative just died, and they want a burial site."

"Here?"

He nodded. "In fact, they said that if I didn't give them a site, they were going to leave the body on our porch."

"Charles!" she gasped.

"Are they going to put a dead man on the porch?" I asked.

"No, no. It's a bluff. It's their way of getting us to do something. Supposedly they can't afford to take him back home."

"Well, I can understand why they're upset," Mom replied, "but we can't do that for every patient that dies. Maybe Marie's right. Maybe we need to be more clear about some rules."

"Kathryn!"

"Well, it's just an idea."

"Whose idea?"

When she didn't answer, he went on: "That's just what she's after. One more person on her side. One more for the nurse. One less for the doctor."

Mom sighed, and the two of them left it there. I was surprised because they almost never disagreed in front of us. It made me curious about Nurse Marie, whom I had talked to only briefly at our Sunday services.

I got my first real chance to see Marie in action a few days later when I convinced Dad to bring me along to see what he did at the hospital. We entered at the foot of the cross-shaped building, which meant passing through the outpatient clinic, where people lined the walls on benches. A cluster of family members stood around a pale-brown woman with a skull-like face. They all turned to watch as we passed by, but the sick woman kept looking at the same spot on the far wall, inhaling loudly as if siphoning air through a hose.

We went down a dark corridor past a room where one of Dad's trainees, an Ethiopian dresser in a blue robe, looked up from counting pills. Dad introduced me as his son, then took me past a sterilizing room where another dresser was using tongs to lift glass syringes out of a steaming autoclave. We passed a closed door with the placard LINENS and another labeled X-RAY. Everything was dark and quiet and gave off sharp odors: alcohol, ammonia, Clorox. The other workers who met us greeted us quietly, respectfully. They echoed my name — *Timotheus* — as Dad introduced me. "*Betam taruno*," they whispered, repeating it in hushed tones — "Very good. Very good." — as if we all understood we must get on to more important business.

Dad turned off the main corridor and passed through double doors into a large, open hall that had six or eight beds lined against the wall. This wing of the cross-shaped building was one of the patient wards. He leaned over the first bed, where a wailing girl was raising her partially wrapped hands and arms as if not sure what to do with them. The child, a four-year-old, had fallen into an open cooking fire, tipping over a pot of boiling water. A dresser was seated next to her, lifting sticky yellow strips of gauze out of an autoclave and gently placing them on the girl's blistered skin.

"Good morning, Yonas," Dad said to the man. He told me that Yonas had just arrived from the Soddo area, where he had worked with Dr. Barlow and the Andersons and all the other people we used to know. Yonas smiled, glad to be acknowledged this way, and he went on working even though the girl clamped her eyes shut and howled. Dad explained that they had to change the bandages every day to avoid infections — that it was the only way to help her heal. He said he would be putting new skin on her arms in a few days.

My eyes watered, and I wondered if I really wanted to be here. I stepped back a few paces.

"How will you put skin on her arms?" I asked. Dad reminded me of the procedure Dr. Barlow used at Soddo to heal elephant foot — how Dr. Barlow would take fresh skin off the person's hips to replace the bad skin. Dad was planning to do the same: to take thin sheets of skin off of this girl's hips with something like the wire cheese-cutter we had in our kitchen, just enough to help new skin grow on her arms.

As we stood watching the bandaging procedure, Nurse Marie stepped into the ward. She was dressed in her all-white uniform and starched cap, with white hose and white shoes and no-nonsense black hair that had been cut close so that it stayed out of her eyes and ended with a single curl at her neck. She didn't seem to see Dad, focusing on me instead and asking what I thought: did I want to become a doctor some day?

"Maybe," I said, smiling shyly.

She looked over at Yonas, who was wrapping up the excess

gauze and collecting the scissors and autoclave. "Boy," she said, trying to get his attention.

I glanced at Dad. His face had contorted. He looked like he might blurt out something, but his jaw was clamped too tightly and, before he could react, Marie had gone on, speaking calmly, stating her demands: "As soon as you finish, I need a thermometer. Bring some alcohol too."

She turned to the bed of the nearest patient and reached for his wrist. Then she turned back toward me, all brightness, and asked, as if we were actors in a play, "So, Doctor, what treatment do you prescribe for my patient?"

I looked behind her at the elderly man who lay there without a shirt. His brown skin was pulled taut over the ridges of his ribs, and he coughed as if his lungs were an empty barrel. The man spat in a metal cup, and I looked to my father, wondering what to say. Dad's face was a mask.

"I don't know," I finally said. "I don't know what's wrong with him."

Marie guffawed. She laughed more loudly than I thought was warranted, making me glance over her shoulder at the hollow-sounding man. "Smart doctor," she proclaimed. "You catch on quickly!"

I didn't see Marie again until that Sunday, our last Sunday before returning to Bingham Academy. When we all met for worship, this time it was at the nurse's house instead of our house or the Dyes's. We followed the usual routine. We read a passage from the Bible and heard a reflection on it from Mr. Dye. We prayed through a list of needs and concerns, checking them off mentally: the girl with the burned arms, the tuberculosis patient who was showing interest in the Gospel of Mark after hearing it on audiotape, the Canadian minister who would teach a special course at the Bible school in Jimma, the people who were complaining that they would leave their relative on our porch, and finally someone's relative back in America who had just announced a divorce.

Mom and Dad and the other adults were so serious about this prayer time that it might as well have been a board meeting. They focused entirely on "the work." To talk about personal depression, frustration, or anxiety seemed taboo. When it was our turn, as children, to throw in requests, I admitted, "I need help not to get angry." The adults smiled and nodded, amused by this break in protocol. Then they went right back to business. What about the English dentist who had returned home to be treated for cancer? Was there any report on his condition?

The one exception to our general solemnity was the songs. A few were too plaintive for me, like the old hymn that began "Beneath the cross of Jesus I fain would take my stand." However, I joined in heartily with the camp song that Mom and Dad had learned as youth workers in the States. It was a sweet, rippling melody that we had often sung at home:

> *In God's green pastures feeding,*
> *By His cool waters lie,*
> *Soft in the evening*
> *Walk my Lord and I.*

I loved the way the women and girls began the refrain, singing the high words — "waters cool" — and then how we males swept in with a lower phrase — "in the valley." I loved the layering of our voices — how they would sing "Pastures greeeeeen" and hold that high note while we completed their thought — "on the mountain."

I also liked how we all stayed after worship to eat lunch. Before the meal we stood in a circle and sang again. Everyone held hands, even Marie and Dad, who looked very sober as they joined into the Doxology: "Praise God from whom all blessings flow."

Then all the children rushed to the table, trying to be first in line. We ate fried chicken and mashed potatoes — two of my favorites. And at the end of the main course, Nurses Marie and Chris brought out a special treat, saying that they had made it in honor of Johnathan and me and Mary Dye and her sister Ruthie, all back from boarding school. They came around with an icy-sided metal canister, tipping it so that we could see inside.

We hooted when we looked in. Lime sherbet!

The parents applauded too, glad to be united by something other than work. Then we all set to, scooping the dessert out of our bowls and holding our spoons upside down so that we could savor the rare coldness, the crisp tartness melting on our tongues. We sang the praises of our hosts, Nurse Chris and Nurse Marie, the sherbet queens. And Marie, usually so efficient, so matter-of-fact, gave us an unguarded smile, happy for a moment simply to cause pleasure.

Sent Back

ALL THROUGH VACATION, Bingham Academy was at the back of my mind, drawing closer. Although I didn't want to contemplate my return to school, I knew that it would happen, and I hated it because it could not be avoided.

On the day of departure, Johnathan and I were taken to Hosanna at sunrise, the Land Rover lurching down roads slick with rain and rusty mud. The Dyes came too. An unexpected deluge had struck overnight, though it was the middle of the dry season. Fog shrouded the countryside. Farmers emerged from the mist in pieces, their white wraparound shawls hiding their torsos so that their legs and arms and shouldered hoes all seemed like separately swinging units.

I was glad for this fog. I thought that maybe it would shroud the soaked airstrip outside Hosanna so that the flight from Addis couldn't land. However, as soon as we reached the one-room, tin-walled airport, a breeze lifted the dirty yellow windsock that dangled on a pole. The fog began to billow and tear, scattering down the valley and exposing the green fields and the big humpback oxen grazing around bushes. We heard a DC-3 droning in the clouds, and we knew our sentence would stand: twelve more weeks away from home.

As Johnathan and I waited to board the plane, the sky began to spit rain. Mom put us in yellow plastic raincoats and gave us peppermints, reminding us to eat them when the plane took off so our ears wouldn't pop. Nat begged for a candy too, so she gave him one. Meanwhile, Dad tried to be cheerful. He talked about how they would visit us, probably six weeks from now. He promised we would do something special in Addis, like going to see the lions at the Emperor's palace.

Johnathan and I had nothing to say. Mute, we followed the Dye girls into the aluminum fuselage of the DC-3. Our suitcases were tossed onto a giant stack at the back of the plane where every imaginable type of cargo was lashed down, even a motorcycle and a crate of chickens.

Canvas bucket seats ran the length of the plane, and only two were left after the girls sat down, so Johnathan and I took our po-

HOSANNA AIRSTRIP.
Waiting for the flight to boarding school.

sitions across the aisle from each other, like paratroopers. Mom and Dad peered in from the gangplank. They tried to bring Nat to us, so they could say goodbye one last time, but Nat strayed too near to one of the passengers — a stern young man with disarrayed hair who threw his legs out, blocking the aisle. This man was being held tightly at both elbows by his relatives but managed to swing his legs at Nat and knock him down. He muttered and kept trying to slide-tackle my brother, who clambered into Dad's arms.

"*Ibbed,*" the relatives offered as their apology — using the Amharic term for "crazy."

He certainly seemed crazy. He wouldn't look at any of us, not even the target of his hostility, and as he took another swipe with his leg, he continued a private conversation with himself, mumbling in Hadiya. The engines started, and the stewardess put a hand on Mom's arm. Nat was crying in a silent panic, afraid that he might be trapped on the plane with this crazy man.

"Fasten your seat belts," Dad called.

"Love you," Mom added, blowing kisses down the aisle between all the Ethiopian strangers. Then they retreated down the gangplank.

The stewardess tugged the curved doors shut and locked them with the flat metal handle. Out the porthole behind me, I could see the fat propellers chopping the air. They growled and sent out a white mist. And through that mist I could see Mom and Dad, still waving. Nat too.

I didn't want to wave back. Mom wiped at her eyes and Dad cinched her up to his side, squeezing her around the shoulders. She looked so sad, at last, that I eventually did wave, but inside I was wondering, *If you don't like it either, then why do I have to go?* I felt angry and, at the same time, guilty for being angry. Most of all I felt helpless because my parents seemed so helpless, at the mercy of something larger than all of us.

As the plane lifted off the runway, I was still turned to the window, staring down at the diminishing specks that were my family — the blue dad dot and the red-and-white mom dot and the bright yellow plastic dot that was Nat — until the heavy gray clouds took over and all I could see were the blurred propellers. The plane shimmied. It bucked. It hit an air pocket and dropped, but when it slammed to a stop on a shelf of air fifty feet below, I kept going right to the floor. My bucket seat had collapsed.

All the Ethiopian passengers laughed, enjoying this unexpected entertainment. They shouted advice in Hadiya and Amharic. Jonathan yelled too, but I couldn't hear him over the engines. I somehow pulled the seat frame erect, but the plane plummeted once more, dumping me on my bottom, legs outstretched.

Now the man next to me reached over and pulled roughly at the framework of the seat. It was jammed in a half-up, half-down position, so he gave up. I did too. I just twisted around, hanging onto the window frame and propping myself against the wall of the plane. I felt in my pocket for the piece of candy Mom had given me, but I found no comfort there. My stomach and throat seemed clamped tight, as if banded with iron straps. I couldn't swallow. I stared out the window into the gray murk, knowing that Mom and Dad and Nat were probably grinding home in the Land Rover. Which direction though?

Water drops strung their way across the window. I watched them stretch and break. But when I looked down, I could see nothing of the ground: not my family, not their little purple house, not even the long white hospital with its two halls shaped like a cross.

And I'll Fly Away

IN MY TIME AWAY from the school, I'd forgotten about its few attractions. Bingham Academy had a small playground with a jungle gym of fitted pipes — smooth pipes that smelled of sweaty palms and old coins. We liked to rub crushed eucalyptus leaves on our fingers to make them sticky, then hang from the bars for as long as possible. More enticing, though, was the nearby woodpile, a grassless yard littered with woodchips and torn logs. When no adults were around, Danny Coleman and I scooted over there. We burrowed into the high piles of split wood. We stacked short pieces into fortlike enclosures, sometimes dragging whole logs into place as roofs. When we emerged, we did it quickly, grabbing the necessary materials then diving back into our den. We knew the teachers wouldn't approve. If they saw us, they would shout us out, afraid of a collapse or someone getting bonked by a log.

On the day Stan Evans approached the woodpile, escorted by our principal, Danny and I spied on him through the cracks in our newest tunnel, wondering what crime he had committed. If an older boy broke the rules, everyone knew because he appeared here, sawing or chopping. We kids could estimate the seriousness of the crime by how long the boy labored. Anything longer than a week, and he was guilty of a major transgression.

Day after day Stan came back, serving out his sentence. The

firm set of his brow, the rigidity of his mouth, the unnecessarily hard way that he struck the logs with the ax, all suggested that maybe he had his own sense of what was right and wrong, and that his standard had not been realized.

He flung the cut logs onto our fort, where they thudded and clonked like incoming shells. Danny and I grinned, happy to be under attack. Deep in the woodpile like rabbits in a warren, we inhaled the rich scent of cut wood — the clean, mentholated odor of torn eucalyptus or the thick, pungent aroma of acacia. We had disappeared from the world as we knew it and entered another realm. We had become much bigger and stronger and more prepared to face our fate: pioneers in a stockade, knights in a castle, soldiers in a foxhole.

Stan ripped and hacked at a long log, effectively reducing the whole tree into pieces small enough to fit through the one-foot-wide porthole on the wood-burning heater behind our dorm. Tonight his efforts would scald the germs from our dirtied dinner plates. Tomorrow they would warm us in the showers. We played, but we played in the wreckage of that anger.

Soon everyone knew the facts: Stan had been sentenced to a month's labor in the woodpile plus a leather strapping every evening for five days. The reason? He alone had shown the audacity to run away from Bingham Academy.

Prior to this, Stan had been the butt of jokes. Even we younger boys didn't take him seriously, because we could tell his own classmates didn't. He constantly wore a shocked expression, with eyes that bulged and eyebrows that were raised as if someone were whispering outrages in his ear. His stick-thin limbs swelled to knobs at the joints.

On the back of his head, like a curse, Stan's hair lay flattened in a cowlick. The older boys liked to surprise him, pushing their knuckles into the center of that circle, then twisting as if his head were a top. Once I had even seen another junior-high boy grab Stan by his knobby wrists and swing him over his shoulder just for the sheer pleasure of feeling tough. Stan left the ground easily, light as a bale of cured straw. Then he slammed down on his back and lay still, wearing that frozen, shocked expression. He was so out of breath he couldn't cry. I felt sorry for him, but not sorry enough.

What a surprise, then, to hear that he had had the guts to escape Bingham. Before Stan, I couldn't even conceive of such a thing. Yet Stan had not only imagined it, he had acted on it as well.

The rumor was that he had learned over Christmas vacation how to steer a motorcycle, practicing on his father's Suzuki 100. When he saw an identical motorcycle parked outside the apartment of one of the bachelor teachers, he began to scheme. Remembering that he had been riding all over the hillsides near Jimma — roaring down ravines, popping over ridges, sashaying around wet cow pies — he felt the necessary confidence to hatch his unlikely plot.

I liked to imagine how he did it. He must have wakened before sunrise. Without disturbing any of the other sleeping boys in the bunks next to him, he must have tiptoed down the center of the dim dormitory. Then he would have climbed out the open back window and peeked over the flowering hibiscus, waiting for the *zebunya* to leave the gate on patrol.

I imagined Stan loping across the cinders of the parking lot to the dark door of the faculty apartments, then easing the motorcycle off its stand and pushing it quietly toward the gate. What exquisite awareness he must have felt. The crisp morning air. The sharp tang of eucalyptus smoke coming from cooking fires outside the Bingham campus. The soft crunch of cinders under those tires.

Somehow he worked the bolt loose and eased back a wing of the gate without too much noise, then slipped through and closed the gate before being noticed. Most likely, he pushed the motorcycle to the main road before kicking it to life. How remarkable — to be a thirteen-year-old taking charge of his own destiny. The control must have given Stan a buzz like the little jolt that comes from touching your tongue to the poles of a nine-volt battery.

Ethiopian woodcutters would have shot by as he turned onto

the main road. They were always out there in the morning — those hurried, somber men, wrapped in shawls against the morning chill. They were always making their way to market, switching the rumps of trotting donkeys, little gray creatures that swayed their heads and took quick, knee-popping steps under heaped wood.

I imagined Stan waving at them gaily. That's what I would have done — what any boy would have done — delighted by the speed of the motorcycle and the crazy adrenaline that came from doing something so bold. But maybe then he had to stop at an intersection, and maybe he became frightened because a group of teenagers in their navy-blue school uniforms called out to him. "Hey, *ferengi*, where ar-ra you going?"

What would Stan have done? What would I have done?

I pictured him cranking back on the throttle, lifting his foot off the clutch, and roaring away. No one could touch him now. He had wheels. He could move at fifty miles an hour. Forget those boys in their uniforms. Forget Bingham Academy and the kids knuckling his cowlick.

Everyone knew the route Stan had taken out of Addis because the story had been passed from student to student. On the other side of town, he had turned down a side road, taking a shortcut that the staff used when they shuttled us to special events at Good Shepherd, the Lutheran boarding school. Over there, fist-sized river rocks cobbled the road, with potholes and ruts between them. Stan had to pick his way through the rubble carefully, sometimes bumping over buried boulders or lurching into holes, but he knew he would be less noticeable this way, harder to track. He was so close to leaving the city. A mere mile, and he would be into the open, headed toward his parents' station, 120 miles west of Leimo.

Maybe he started thinking about the countryside and the road in front of him, a road he had traveled a dozen times back and forth from Bingham. I had heard about the Jimma road from another boy my age, one who used to live at the station there. It was a wonderful twisting road which peaked at seven or eight thousand feet, almost a mile and a half above sea level in the cold, misty mountains, with drop-offs where African kites sailed alongside, never flapping, their trim wings outstretched and only their tails twisting, like rudders in the wind.

But whatever Stan was thinking as he took that pitted side street, his thoughts must have evaporated when the handlebars went sluggish in his hands. The bike jolted unusually hard, so he glanced down. His front tire was flat.

According to the rumors, that was as far as Stan got. He was halted right there on the edge of Addis, tantalizingly close to the open road. Once again, he became a thirteen-year-old, constrained by the limits of his age.

I felt sure that a crowd gathered. Crowds always gathered around *ferengi* children like us — especially if we were unescorted. And if they gathered, they would have thrown questions at Stan, speaking in Amharic. He might have acted as if he didn't know their language. He might have tried to hang onto his alternate picture of reality by shutting them out. Yet I know Stan had been in Ethiopia long enough to understand almost every word they said:

"Boy, where did you get that motorcycle?"

"Where are you going?"

"Hey you, does your father know you are here?"

"Are you deaf?"

"Are you asleep?"

"Are all of you white children like this?"

"Are you part donkey?"

The panicked faculty spread out across Addis, stopping pedestrians to ask if they had seen a white boy on a motorcycle. Maybe the woodcutters tipped them off, or the Ethiopian students nodded yes, they had seen a little *ferengi*. He went that way.

When I thought about Stan waiting with the crippled motorcycle, that was the part that hurt the worst. That was the part that brought back my own helplessness — the paralysis that spread from my chest to my extremities each time I was left at Bingham Academy. What might his parents say? He probably could have endured any response if only he had gotten to their house on his own terms, as a youth who had taken charge of his destiny like a man. Instead, now he would have to hear it on everyone else's terms — as still-a-boy.

The laughing voices of the Ethiopian crowd, some of them children younger than Stan, must have rung in his ears. I imagined him getting ready to pitch the motorcycle into the ditch and walk away, headed toward the distant mountains. However, before he could steel himself for such an action, a Land Rover bore down on the crowd. The school principal climbed out, frowning. Without a word, the grim man pulled the handlebars from Stan, then shoved the motorcycle to the back gate of the vehicle and began to hoist it. Stan's journey was over.

For thirty afternoons after that, Stan worked in the woodpile. Beside him, burrowing in the growing pile of split logs, Danny and I were at work in our own way, building make-believe fortresses and escape tunnels, safely hidden from prying eyes. Sometimes I nearly fell asleep in the tunnels, where sunlight settled in odd patches on the sawdust and across my torso, warming my flannel shirt. I could hear the muffled clump of the ax, which roused me. I whispered to Danny, "Let's pretend we're Daniel Boone and Davy Crockett and the Indians are out there. If we stay completely quiet, no one will find us." I would imagine my way out of Bingham or, instead, turn inward until I was so buried I was gone.

We could see Stan through the cracks in our cavern, lifting the man-sized ax, then striking it down with a clap. One log, then the next, then the next. I noticed that the older kids who walked by weren't laughing at his cowlick now, or his knobby arms. He didn't avert his eyes when he looked back, not even when the staff walked past. He stared at them defiantly. According to the school rules, what he had done was wrong. He had even broken a commandment: do not steal. But as Stan chopped those logs in the woodpile, I watched from my hiding place and, with each swing of the ax, he earned my admiration.

What Kind of Children?

ONE AFTERNOON, tired of make-believe, Danny and I turned to hunting. Our attempts to bag a bird took us all over the woods at the back of the school compound. Down on our hands and knees, we crawled toward a fat, glossy pigeon. It strolled and pecked at the bare ground under a low-lying pine, close to the boarding school fence. It lifted its head, straining its iridescent neck so that the blue and green sheen of its feathers rippled like poured oil.

In my fist, I clenched a little club that I had fashioned by rubbing a eucalyptus root on the cement tuck-pointing of the administrative building. When the bird lowered its head again, I lifted this crude weapon and pulled it back slowly, as if my arm were a shadow moving with the sun. I rose to my knees, patient as plant growth. This was not a Malachite Kingfisher like the ones I had spotted at the Leimo stream, or a mousebird like the ones in the avocado tree at Soddo. This was an ordinary pigeon of the sort I saw every day at Bingham, and I wanted to kill it.

With a dull *thump,* a rock bounced on the ground next to the pigeon, which panicked. It whacked through the needled canopy of the pine and shot away over the school fence, clapping its wings.

"Aw, I had it," I yelled.

"Me too," Danny echoed.

"My friend, how ar-ra you?" came a voice from the other side of the fence. We ignored this taunt, too mad to give the speaker even the slight satisfaction of looking in his direction.

Thump. A second rock landed near our feet.

"You, my friend. Whad-dis your name?"

Now we *did* look, and we saw a boy almost twice our size, with one hand on the chain-link fence, grinning. He held a rock in the other hand. From the tall grass at his feet a smaller boy appeared, lifting his head slowly and staring at us. He rose to his knees in imitation of our hunting motions, drew back his arm, and faked a throw.

"*Mininit lidgeoch,*" Danny shouted, scolding the boys with the question that Ethiopian adults so often used on misbehaving kids: "What kind of children are you?"

"You, my friend," replied the standing boy. "Come to me now!"

The other one, still on his knees, bowed his head and reached to his eyes. When he looked up again, both eyelids were folded back, so that they showed slick and orange above the eyeballs, raw as cut meat.

"I've had it," I said, emboldened by Danny and by the knowledge that these boys were on the other side of the fence. No Ethiopian boys would come inside. They didn't dare. I picked up the rock at our feet and lobbed it back, where it clanked into the chain links and sent a metallic shiver down the fence.

The Ethiopian boys were galvanized into action, as if this was the thing they had been waiting for all along. They scooped up rocks and slung them over the fence, one, two, three at a time, so that they rained down through the leaves and the pine needles.

"Let's get out of here," Danny yelled, and we raced away, zigzagging separate courses up the hill to the playground.

"They could have killed us," he gasped.

"Did you see me? I dodged one or it would have hit me right in the back."

"That's nothing. I almost got hit in the head."

We were anxious but excited. What had started as imaginary

play was now real. "Wanna go back and see if they're gone?" I asked.

"Yeah. We better."

Back we crept through the forest, hugging the ground, slithering up to bushes, making quick dashes from one tree trunk to the next. When we reached the spot where everything had happened, we were disappointed to see that the fence was bare, the rough road empty.

"Maybe they're hiding by the river," I said, and we went farther down the fence, to where it bent back along the edge of a steep ravine, not far from the cave where Danny and I had first met our "girlfriends." We didn't see the Ethiopian boys, but to our surprise we found two older Bingham boys, about the same age as our antagonists, who were hunting with slingshots. Like us, they crept softly on the ground, careful not to snap a twig, keeping bushes and trees between them and their prey. They got down on hands and knees and eased up to the fence line, looking down at whatever lay hidden below, down by the yellow stream. We dropped to the ground, excited by this new possibility — to hunt the hunters.

What was it they were looking at? I could hear the light babble of Amharic, the splashing of water, the slap of wet cloth against boulders. Apparently, a group of women were down there washing clothes.

One of the Bingham boys pulled back the pouch on his slingshot, pinching the rock tightly until it was in firing position next to his cheek. He lifted his shooting arm, then released, letting the front hand flip down to add impetus. The rock flew high and silent, rising fifty feet above the fence, then arcing down and disappearing into the ravine.

"Aiee!"

The scream of a woman, so sudden and startling in the silence of the late afternoon, paralyzed Danny and me, but the two older boys leapt to their feet and fled. They had been spotted. I heard female voices calling after them in rage: "*Mininit lidgeoch!*"

Now we belly crawled to the fence and lifted our heads just high enough to see. A cluster of women was gathered around a stricken comrade, who slumped by the water with her hand pressed to her forehead. Blood dribbled out from under her palm, a rivulet that spattered off her brow and blossomed bright red on the gray cloth of her worn dress. She rocked from side to side. The women lifted the hand away to see the swollen gash, then pressed it back with a wet cloth.

One looked up toward us, saw the golden thatch of Danny's hair, and called out in Amharic. We needed no translation. We, the devil children, were already bear-walking away, wanting not to be identified. When we were far enough to not be seen, we galloped.

It did not take long for the washerwomen to arrive at the entrance to Bingham Academy, bringing along a dozen irate friends. A small mob pounded on the tin gate, screaming for attention. Danny and I watched from the concrete ramp of our dorm, afraid to get closer but too curious to hide. The *zebunya* opened the gate a crack, clutching his cudgel, and the women spilled through.

What if one of them recognized Danny and me? I took a few steps up the ramp toward the dorm, tugging at his arm. But the women were too busy reacting to the guard's threats to even look around. They had become a milling cacophony centered on the old man. "*Woosha,*" they shouted, insulting him with the label "dog." They took the bloody bandage from the woman's forehead to point at her egglike lump.

By now, other children had come running, along with an Ethiopian gardener and one of the school's paid drivers. Danny and I followed the crowd. At the windows of the dining hall, all the Ethiopian staff were watching too. Some had even stepped outside. Our principal emerged from the kitchen entrance and jogged across the red cinders in his white shirt and tie, sandy hair rising like a crest on his head. With him he brought the head cook, who began an uneasy negotiation, working from the *zebunya*'s translation of what the women wanted. Mr. Wallace responded in English, letting the cook explain. The women eyed them both suspiciously, throwing out their hands. "Do you see what they have done?" one seemed to ask as she turned toward all of us standing in a half-circle gaping.

This spokeswoman was beautiful in a wild, hardened way. She had flat cheeks and high, carved cheekbones, and a bright white head cloth wound around her head. Next to that white wrap, her skin glowed dark brown like oiled walnut.

"*Mininit lidgeoch?*" she asked, her eyes flitting from face to face.

Danny had turned toward me, and I was trying not to look back, not to appear connected. We didn't do anything; we just saw it happen. Besides, it was an accident, wasn't it?

I glanced behind me at the staff of Bingham, but that was even more disturbing than looking at the woman. The staff were all so attentive. They were no longer a backdrop I ignored as I lived out my days at the school, no longer reduced to their roles: clothes washer, guard, driver, grass cutter. Their gaze expressed a sadness that weighed heavily on me.

I stared down at the cinders, then glanced at the head cook, who was still trying to interpret for Mr. Wallace. When the cook looked at us, his eyes seemed hard as marbles. Whatever he was hearing from the shouting women had stolen away the smile we were accustomed to, the pleasant face that he put on when he came skating across the wooden floor with platters of food.

Mr. Wallace must have felt this change in the other man and in the watching staff, because now he said, "Tell her this is not the time or place to be talking. If she can come back, we will talk in private and find a way to resolve the problem."

The woman spat when she heard the translation, as though clearing her mouth of a bad taste. She launched into a terrific tirade, aiming all her fury at the head cook. He tried to interrupt her, but she just shouted over him.

"What is she saying?" asked Mr. Wallace.

For a moment, the cook forgot his role. He waved Mr. Wallace away, as if the principal were an Ethiopian boy in the street, a child who had made the mistake of interrupting. Then he remembered himself, looked confused, almost frightened. He stammered. "She is . . . What she says . . . is not so good to tell you."

"Why? Is she threatening us?"

"No. She is talking about the Ethiopians who work here."

"What about them?"

"She says we are all to be ashamed . . ."

"Look. Tell her that this is not the time. We have an injury here. Let's have the woman treated. Our nurse can take care of her."

Before the head cook could translate, the impatient woman stooped down and picked up a handful of cinders. She swirled and swung her arm at us children. We scattered, feeling the sting of the tiny rocks. When we looked back, the woman's companions had grabbed her. They pulled her toward the gate. They pointed at the injured woman, who had sat down on the cinders. The school nurse stepped forward, and it was over.

That evening, after the protesters had been escorted away, we ate dinner served by a strangely quiet kitchen staff. Mr. Wallace made an announcement: "If anyone knows how the woman got hit by a rock at the river, then I want to know. This is a serious matter, so you need to speak up."

I stared at his tie as he talked, because I was afraid of his eyes. I knew I should go to him. I knew that a good Christian would take on this responsibility — the responsibility of doing what was right. But it felt so large and heavy. I didn't want to carry it. I didn't want to think about it anymore. Instead I followed Danny and my classmates out the door and ran across the cinders to my dorm.

Rain had just begun to patter down. This was the first real rain of the new wet season, and when it reached full strength, it cascaded out of the sky and clattered on the tin roof of the dorm until the building roared. That night, I couldn't sleep with all the insistent hammering. I lay in bed, buried under the sound.

The next morning I had to be shaken by Mrs. Johnson. But once awake, I sat up quickly, because I heard all my dormmates exclaiming as if they had spotted a rainbow. They stood at the window in their PJs and underwear, and when I joined them, I saw why. Flying termites had surfaced from the soaked ground. They were airborne all over the school grounds, fluttering through the trees, ricocheting off of walls, resting on roofs. They banged into us as we crossed the parking lot to verse group. On the ground, the tired ones tangled and bit away each other's wings, which floated loose across the cinders.

After breakfast, Mrs. Johnson reminded us that it was laundry day and that we needed to go back across the parking lot to deliver our dirty clothes before class. I took mine in a blue-jeans bag slung over my shoulder. At Gowan Hall, I followed my classmates down a set of cement stairs where termite wings had gathered in little drifts. Coming up the steps was the blond eighth-grader who shot the woman with his slingshot. This reminded me of the secret I still carried inside. He appeared so normal, so unaffected, that I didn't understand why my body tensed after seeing him. Why did it feel hard to walk?

Uneasy, I stepped through the sunken door into a long room where light bulbs hung in a row. I tossed my bag onto a pile. Damp granules of soap dotted the floor and rose in little clumps like white molehills. From the wires overhead, wet sheets dangled, translucent where they draped against themselves.

Since the rains made outdoor drying nearly impossible, the laundry women were hanging everything inside. They worked on both sides of the hanging lines, squatting on stools. They heaped the sour clothing into galvanized tubs, stirring a roiling stew. It was a dirty stew, gray with the dust of the playground and the salt of our sweat, with spilled porridge and flecks of snot. It slopped and smacked. It splattered as they lifted each article, wringing it into thick rope: blue-jeans rope and white T-shirt rope and red sweatshirt rope. Untwisted, the clothes were slung over the wires, where they hung down, dripping so loudly that the rain seemed to have moved inside.

The other boys left, and the laundresses didn't look up. They went on speaking in their quiet Amharic, sorting clothes and throwing them into the tubs. One woman noticed, though, that I was still standing by the main laundry pile. She was wearing a tight blue turban like my nanny Marta used to wear at our station in the south. She was older, with a mouth that turned down at the corners and brows that seemed to pinch together in a questioning manner. She stopped talking to her comrade and spoke to me in Amharic: "*Mindino?*"

"What do you want?" is what she asked. But I didn't know what I wanted, or how to say it, and when she saw that I didn't know, she was amused. She smiled, revealing teeth that were twisted, overlapped.

She pointed at me to come. I stepped forward, but she clucked and gestured for me to bring the bag I had added to the pile. I lifted the bag and carried it to her. She smiled as though she was pleased with me or pleased with herself — I couldn't tell which. As I handed her the bag, the woman on the stool next to her stifled a laugh, causing me to step back. Still the crooked-toothed woman held me with her eyes. She did not acknowledge the laughter. She wiped her hand on her apron and extended it, American-style, smiling that same enigmatic smile, her brows pulled together.

"Whaddis your name?"

I was not sure if she was fooling with me, so I was slow to respond. She jiggled her hand impatiently, so I took it, feeling repulsed by the damp, wrinkled skin. She didn't shake, but she didn't let go either, and now the laundress on the next stool laughed again, as if this was the finest entertainment she had had in weeks.

The woman with the crooked teeth stared into my eyes, waiting. I remembered her question.

"Tim," I said. "My name is Tim."

"*Mindino?*" she asked, wanting more clarity.

"*Timotheus,*" I said, and finally her pinched brows relaxed, lifting with recognition.

"*Ahhh. Timotheus.*" She repeated the Ethiopian version confidently. This ancient name was familiar. It was a name given to priests in the Coptic church, a name that could be found in any Amharic translation of the Bible.

"*Betam taruno,*" she said, meaning that it was a good name, a name to be proud of.

I was pleased that we had this small connection — this single word we both understood — although I was not sure it summed me up the way she wanted to sum me up. I did not feel as good as my name. I kept remembering the bleeding woman by the river, and the angry one flinging the cinders, and Mr. Wallace saying, "This is a serious matter. You need to speak up."

The woman with the crooked teeth had not let go of my hand. She held it firmly in her damp, wrinkled hand, as if I was hers until she decided. As she allowed herself a quick glance at her companion, I pulled free, then bolted for the stairs. I took them two at a time, with termite wings fluttering around my feet, lifting in little clouds. Behind me I could hear both women clucking with disapproval. They had not given me permission to leave. I should turn back. A boy named *Timotheus* would know better. A boy named *Timotheus* would do the right thing.

My Pilgrim Progress

OF ALL THE DAYS of the boarding school week, Sunday seemed worst: the day of rest and the day of reckoning. After breakfast, the seventh-, eighth-, and ninth-graders climbed into vans and rode away to church five kilometers across the city, but we grade-schoolers shuffled off to assigned meeting rooms. Those staff members who hadn't gone to church at headquarters gathered us by age level for an hour and a half of religious education. We watched desultory flannelgraph stories from the Bible, full of saintly models, then listened to entreaties about the state of our souls. We closed our eyes and prayed, concentrating so hard that vertigo took over. The teachers seemed so concerned about this invisible reality — the soul — that I experienced an urgent need to reform mine. But how? What could I do to improve something I couldn't even see?

When Sunday school was over and the fleet of VW vans buzzed back through the academy gate, the older kids spilled out and we got a brief reprieve: lunchtime. Then came the most dreaded part of the day: "Rest Hour."

Nothing could be more excruciating than this enforced period of silence. I could neither fall asleep nor talk, and so I was unable to ignore my thoughts. Between one and three on Sunday afternoon I couldn't escape the hard fact that my parents and younger brother lived hundreds of miles away or that my older brother, though within shouting distance, was locked in his own dormitory cell. I also couldn't turn to Danny or my roommates for companionship. I had no option but to take stock of myself—to contemplate how alone I was.

That first year at the academy, after rainy season began, Rest Hour was often accompanied by a downpour. Rain drummed on the tin roof, and I lay there on the lower level of my bunk bed, aware that five other boys were lying on their own mattresses—one right above me—and yet we were all in our own separate spaces thinking our own separate thoughts. Only when this heavy silence had settled on the room fully, like wet cement, would I hear Mrs. Johnson coming down the hall clapping her hands: "Everyone up now. Put on your church clothes. Fifteen minutes till chapel."

We rose quietly and did an awkward dance in our underwear, our thin torsos hopping and jerking as we pulled on black dress pants and white dress shirts, as we clipped on bow ties tight as choke collars and wrestled our arms into black suit jackets stiff as stove pipe. A room full of seven-year-olds donning their Puritan armor.

Once dressed, we shuffled into the hallway and followed Mrs. Johnson out the dorm ramp, heads heavy with half-sleep and private thought. If the rains had not let up, we opened black umbrellas and marched out under them. For a moment, we stood beside the little chain-link gate at the entrance to the school chapel while Mrs. Johnson pulled us into a proper line. Then we filed into the boxlike building with the dusty yellow windowpanes, a building that stood mysteriously empty for so much of the week that it smelled vacant even after we occupied it.

We called our Sunday-afternoon service "Loyal Ambassadors for Christ," or L.A.C. And the song we sang as we shuffled to our designated pews could not have been more fitting for us as loyal ambassadors: "Onward, Christian soldiers, marching as to war, with the cross of Jesus going on before." Every Sunday that tune ripped a hollow in my chest. A soldier indeed. If so, then I was conscripted, not voluntary. I sang in the mumbling half-whisper that kids adopt when their hearts aren't in the music. Sometimes I merely mouthed the words. However, even though I refused to make the song mine, it swirled around me. I couldn't get away from it: "Forward into battle, see his banners go. Onward, Christian soldiers, marching as to war."

The spiritual vacuum of those Sunday chapel services stayed unrelieved until halfway through the second semester of second grade, when the teacher from the grade ahead of us — who was really a rather nice, matter-of-fact lady with a husky, energetic voice (the sort that cheerleaders get after yelling too long) — met with us and announced that she would be preparing us to perform a play during L.A.C. As Miss Willey began to describe the story that the second grade would act out, I felt the first hint of interest in something "Sunday."

Pilgrim's Progress was the play, based on the allegory by John Bunyan, and she had selected Danny Coleman and me for key roles. I would be Pilgrim, otherwise known as Christian, and she had chosen Danny to be Christian's fellow traveler, Hopeful. Maybe it was our success with verse memorization that had earned us these prime roles. Or maybe it was the way the two of us hung together all the time — like the traveling companions in Bunyan's story. In any case, we relished the opportunity to act alongside each other, and we listened with extra attentiveness when we started to read through the script.

At first, I stumbled over the dense language of the seventeenth-century English, but then I slowly began to comprehend, even to feel, what was happening. Bunyan's story awoke unexpected emotions. First of all, Christian was without a family or home. He had tried to persuade his wife and children to come with him so that they could escape the fire from heaven that would rain down on their city. However, they had refused, convinced that he had gone mad. Desperate, he fled his own house with his family begging him to stop. He plugged his ears and ran on, crying, "Life! Life! eternal life!"

When I read it, I felt heartbroken for them all — a family torn apart by spiritual yearning. And I felt intimidated by the tremendous task that Christian had taken upon himself — to journey all the way from his home in the City of Destruction to the faraway, rumored Mount Zion. I knew what Bunyan meant by Mount Zion — heaven itself. Maybe Christian's wife and children weren't that far off the mark; maybe he really was mad. Columbus had seemed crazy when he ordered his sailors to the edge of the earth, risking a plummet into the abyss. But to walk from one's home to heaven?

One by one, dangers cropped up. The Slough of Despond, where Christian took a single wrong step and nearly sank into oblivion. The Doubting Castle, where the Giant Despair took him prisoner, starved him, beat him mercilessly, telling him that his only freedom lay in killing himself. And worst of all, the gloomy, mist-shrouded Valley of Humiliation, where the monster Apollyon came at him with fish-scale skin and dragon wings, belching fire and slinging burning darts.

What a relief when he finally stepped between the chained lions at the Palace Beautiful. At last, a haven. Four grave and tender sisters came out to greet him: Discretion, Prudence, Piety, and Charity. "Come in, thou blessed of the Lord," they said. He had lost his family, but now he got one back, found himself treated like a brother. The beautiful sisters fed him "fat things and wine" and talked with him all evening, telling him stories of the Lord of the hill, who had built this mansion out of love for pilgrims and who had fought and slain the one who had "the power of death." That night they put him in a large upper chamber whose windows would open on the rising sun, a room they called "Peace." And when he woke, Christian broke into song:

> *Where am I now? Is this the love and care*
> *Of Jesus for the men that pilgrims are.*

At this point in the story, when Miss Willey's voice had almost gone hoarse from reading, I wanted to shout, "Stay, Christian, don't go any further." But of course Christian went on with his epic journey, determined to arrive at his ultimate destination, Mount Zion. And I traveled along in my imagination. First to the City of Vanity Fair, where he was taken prisoner and saw a companion burned at the stake. Then on to the snare of the false angel. And on from one near disaster to the next.

When Miss Willey finally took us to the empty chapel for our dress rehearsal, I felt the magic of my own costume. I donned black dress shoes with belt buckles taped to them, then put on a stiff-brimmed hat of blackened cardboard and hoisted a bag with shoulder straps. Like the pilgrim Christian I had to trudge along under this rucksack. It was a great burlap bag stuffed with boots and balls so that it would bulge. Bigger than the laundry bag I carried to the laundresses each week, it sagged low on my back. For the first half of the play I dragged it from one place to the next, feeling it pulling me back and down, turning each step into work. But then came that pivotal moment on the journey when I stood before a painted two-by-four cross. Because we had rigged a secret way to loosen the bag, I had only to tug on a string hidden in my shirt, and the whole bundle fell to the ground with a *thump*.

That moment, when all the weight dropped away, was a moment of great mystery and beauty for me. I felt lightness in my limbs. I felt almost that I could float free of the floor. Jesus had said, "Come to me you weary and heavy laden," and I had come. Could it really be true? Could all the weight drop away so that I felt what this storybook Christian called "the beginning of my bliss"?

Each time we practiced, I looked forward to that scene: the solidness of the bag dropping away. The tiptoe sense of becoming light. The metaphor of my soul set free. It was a kind of secret acted out in front of everyone, yet all mine.

Even on Sunday when we performed for the school, this moment was my own private pleasure. I relished it so much that I could almost stop the play there. But just like my character, Christian, I had to continue — to finish what had been begun. And so at last, with all the school watching, I reached the final obstacle in Christian's journey: the River of Death.

Danny had joined me on this leg of the journey as the pilgrim Hopeful, and together we waded out into the pale-blue construction-paper river wearing our tinfoil armor — two brave little soldiers, two ambassadors for Christ, loyal to the end. For a moment my faith wavered, and I began to flounder, but Hopeful lifted my head above the paper waves and cried out, "These troubles are no sign that God has forsaken you, but are sent to try you, to see whether you will call to mind the goodness you have received of Him, and live upon Him in your distress."

He held me around the waist and hoisted me to the shore, and at last the two of us made it to the gates of the Celestial City — Zion — where we were truly greeted by "ten thousand welcomes." All the other students applauded, even the old ones. I could see my brother Johnathan with the pew of sixth-grade boys, and even he was clapping, grinning the way older brothers do when they are embarrassed and amused and secretly proud. I had made it. I had walked all the way from earth to heaven.

I floated out the door of the chapel, headed to supper, and stayed aloft through sunset that one Sunday at Bingham. Bunyan's story had done this for me, not theology or doctrine, not even prayer. The story had lifted me out of one realm and deposited me elsewhere. The king's trumpeters saluted. All the bells rang for joy.

At bedtime, I peeled off my black-and-white Sunday armor, then slid between the cool sheets, curling my toes until they cracked. The room had not changed for all the excitement. Four cinderblock walls, dim gray in the dark. A barred window. Iron beds with identical wool blankets. And five other boys, each lost in his own thoughts.

Miss Willey had told us that John Bunyan wrote *Pilgrim's Progress* while he was in jail, treating the story as if it were a dream, and that when he ended the story, he pictured himself waking up still in jail. If he had written the entire story while imprisoned, he must have wakened each morning to the same dank stone walls and the same barred window, still cut off from his children and wife. Twelve years in that closed space. Twelve years of punishment for what he believed — the same number of years a child spends in school. And in those twelve years, Bunyan's only escape was his dreamed journey to Zion.

I rolled over on my pillow, so that I could watch the ghostly leaves of the eucalyptus rattling outside my window in the moonlit breeze. Even if my own release was only a dream, I still felt it. I remembered the burlap bag falling off my back and the wonderful winged feeling that came afterward. I understood why Christian wanted to sing when he woke in the room called Peace. I hoped that in the coming morning I would wake there myself.

The Volcanic Lake

MY DESIRE TO WAKE in peace found a kind of fulfillment not long after our performance of *Pilgrim's Progress*. Mom and Dad sent word by short-wave radio that they were coming and that we would take a weekend away, at Lake Bishoftu. I knew from other missionary children that Bishoftu was like no other place in the whole country. My dormmates cooed with envy when they heard I was going. The way they spoke about the lake was the way Christian spoke of the Palace Beautiful. A haven in the wilderness. An oasis of delight.

How eagerly I waited! On the day itself, I felt none of the strange ambivalence that had come over me at Christmas — probably because this was not a scheduled holiday. It came as an unexpected gift, so I felt unrestrained delight as I climbed into the back seat of the Land Rover beside my two brothers, sinking into the nest of our family. The awful tin gates of the academy screamed on their hinges. Then we passed through, set free.

Johnathan and I rolled down our windows and poked our heads out, mouthing the warm wind. As we left Addis Ababa, we brayed at passing donkeys and waved to shepherd boys. Back and forth, the Land Rover twisted, down the escarpment into an immense valley south of Addis — the great Rift Valley that stretched clear through Kenya to Tanzania. Eons ago this region had been a colossal blister of earth lifted by volcanic activity. Then eruptions and earthquakes had brought it down, collapsing on itself. Lake Bishoftu, our destination, was a remnant of that long-ago tectonic activity, a lake that had formed in the cone of an extinct volcano. The mission had leased a few acres to create their retreat center, and that's where we would stay.

The countryside turned more rocky and barren as we dropped out of the highlands, except for occasional fields that were green or yellow-green with grain. Here and there, women sat on the roadside, sheltered under umbrellas, and they held out tied bunches of chickpeas. Dad stopped to buy a bundle, showing us how to break off the pods and snap them open to expose the sweet nodules inside. These snacks kept us occupied until we arrived in the dusty trucking town of Debre Zeit, with all its billboards for Orange Fanta and the native honey-wine called *tej*.

Dad turned us off the main road and slowed for a donkey cart — a rustic wooden bench and cargo box bolted to the wheeled axle of a truck trailer. We passed more of these carts as we worked our way out of Debre Zeit and into the open fields beyond, where egrets lifted out of the crop rows and sailed away with occasional flaps of their long white wings.

LAKE BISHOFTU.
Johnathan at the oars. Me in the prow. Dad and Nat in the stern.

Finally we topped the crater rim and looked down at the fabled lake. It did not disappoint. A wonderful contrast to the dry, rocky terrain that we had been passing through, Lake Bishoftu rested in the crater like a turquoise plate in a brown bowl. As Mom and Dad went to register at the main building, my brothers and I simply stood by the hot, ticking Land Rover, gazing at the lake and at the compound below us as if it might disappear. The mission had planted flower gardens and wispy pepper trees all along the steep incline, nurturing banks of papery bougainvillea so that the whole slope blossomed purple and rustled in the breeze. Passion fruit vines had transformed wire fences into living walls. Flame trees blazed orange. And hidden amid this carefully kept flora, adobe cabins peeked out of excavated grottoes, painted pastel blue and green and violet.

Our own lime-green cabin, halfway down to the lake, had breezy windows and a screen door that slapped shut enthusiastically. After the enameled cinder blocks of my dormitory at Bingham Academy, it was a genuine pleasure palace. My brothers and I shouted and bounced on the springy beds. However, the lure of the lake was too strong to linger. As soon as we had helped to carry the bags into the cabin, we stripped and pulled on cutoff shorts and raced out the screen door, headed for the boathouse.

Tucked into a crevice between giant slabs of red volcanic basalt, the tin-roofed boathouse rested right on the water. It echoed with little lapping waves and the knocking together of boats. Inflated inner tubes bulged on the walls, along with faded life preservers that smelled wonderfully damp and moldy, like seaweed and frog skin. When Mom and Dad arrived, Johnathan and I lowered ourselves down into the black water, then swam out of this shadowy cavern into the brilliant sparkling lake.

We dove and surfaced inside the ring of a huge tractor inner tube tethered to the dock. We yelped from inside its center hole, enjoying the novelty of being out on the lake but invisible.

"Where are they?" we heard Nat ask, until we poked our hands up and waved.

For a while, we tread water in the black, rubbery middle of the tractor tube, mesmerized by the green light that swam up out of the lake. A current on my legs went from cold to warm, sweeping my skin like an unseen presence. I jerked my legs up. The green submarine light lit my brother's face from below, making it look unnatural. This light seemed to be rising from a source in the depths of the lake. Was the ancient volcano still alive? Was white-hot magma glowing down there, under hundreds of feet of water?

Momentarily frightened, I dove away, struck by the odd feeling that I was swimming in the maw of some immense monster. I slapped and kicked my way to the raft moored nearby, then lunged up the slippery green steps.

Just when I had begun to relax again, I glanced over the side of the raft, and something long and black and shaped like an *S* snapped down into the lake and disappeared only a few yards away.

"Snake!" I yelled.

"Where? Where?" Johnathan yelled as he thrashed toward the raft.

"There," I shouted, shivering as the foot-long *S* suddenly popped up another twenty yards away.

"You doofus," Johnathan laughed. "That's a bird. It's an African Darter."

"I knew that," I said. But I didn't know it. I was just relieved—and intrigued. What a strange creature. A trickster. Now you see me, now you don't.

The darter ducked down again, and I scanned the lake clear to the shore, but I couldn't find it. Had it swum to the reeds? Or was it still underwater, hovering, perhaps swimming back toward us? And how deep did it dive?

Dad paddled up with a canoe, bringing Nat and Mom, so Johnathan and I tumbled in to join them on a tour. Here was another delight—to slip across the water without engine or effort, at least on our part. As Dad paddled, we three boys leaned over the side so that we could look straight down and glimpse an occasional tilapia, flashing silver, then gone. We pulled at the shimmering water and flung handfuls at Mom, who scolded us happily.

After a few minutes, Dad turned us toward the reeds on the lake shore, which reared up as a wall of canes and long tapering leaves. Although Mom protested, he shoved the canoe right into the stuff, so that the thick stalks skittered against the aluminum. Farther in, the reeds parted to reveal a dark hall. Where the ribbony leaves drooped to the water, they completed an arching tunnel.

Dad swung the canoe sideways, and we drifted silently in this unexpected hiding place, with strips of sunlight thrown down on the dark water. A striped weaverbird, yellow and brown like the sunlight and shadows, zipped into the canopy and went to work constructing its upside-down house, knotting together bits of grass. We looked closer and realized that a whole colony of these nests hung down, all of them ball-like except for a hallway entrance that gave them the appearance of igloos upended.

One weaverbird, with yellow breast and striped wings, spurted out of the reeds above our canoe, making its nest bob and squeak.

"There's babies," I whispered. "I can hear them."

Dad reached up with a paddle and pulled down the nest. He peered inside. He put his finger on his lips.

"Let me see," I whispered.

"Me too," my brothers echoed.

We all took turns peeking into the dark interior of the little thatched hut and touching the basketlike sides, which were surprisingly firm and smelled of hay. We could just make out the ugly heads of three chicks, raw and pimply. They pumped their beaks.

"Can we keep them?" I asked.

"Oh, I don't think the mama bird would like that," said Mom.

"Why not?"

"How would they stay alive?"

"I could feed them. Honestly. I could catch bugs and dig up worms and stuff."

"But you don't want the mama to miss her babies."

"I could bring them back after a while, when they got bigger."

She smiled gently and rubbed my crewcut, but Dad had already released the nest. It bounced in the leafy arch above, where we could hear the chicks squeaking with fear or hunger or blind habit.

Unexpectedly, my father clamped my arm and pointed over the prow of the canoe. There, in the striped shadows, the African Darter had emerged, still and alert. Its dagger-shaped beak and slender neck were raised a foot out of the water, giving off the faintest ripple. Almost all of its slender body was submerged except for a strip of pinstriped feathers on its back. How long had it been there, spying on us, I wondered.

Dad fanned his paddle cautiously and we slid closer, frozen into bird-watching mannequins, until I could see the liquid pupil of the darter's eye — like a bulging drop of oil in its satchel of red skin — and the sharp beak, black and hard as obsidian. Then, *ploop*, the beak and the sinuous neck withdrew, leaving only circles in the water.

Dad paddled mightily, shooting the canoe out of the reedy tunnel.

"Charles!" Mom shrieked as leaves smacked at us.

"There it goes," Johnathan called.

Our father dug harder, pulling so forcefully that Nat tipped over and rolled in the puddled basin of the canoe.

"Go, Dad, go," Johnathan and I chanted.

"This is not a good idea," Mom warned, palming Nat's worried face. "Besides, it's almost supper time."

"No problem," Dad grunted.

The darter was scooting along like a little raised submarine. We could see the inverted knees of its black legs pumping like piston shafts. We pulled within ten yards. Then five. Johnathan lay down on the prow, stretching out both arms.

"Johnathan! Get back," Mom commanded.

"But we're going to catch it," I exclaimed. "I know it."

The darter, for some reason, seemed incapable of flight, which is why I thought we really *might* catch it. But part of me secretly hoped we wouldn't. That beak, that red-rimmed eye: I didn't want to get too close.

Johnathan reached. The canoe wobbled. Then the darter was gone. Its dagger bill speared into the lake. The slippery torpedo of its body followed, legs tucked in. Nothing remained but a small circular wake.

Dad stopped paddling and heaved for air. We boys scanned the sleek skin of the lake, each hoping to be the first to spot a rip — a signal that the darter had sliced back to the surface. However, after a full twenty seconds, we still hadn't found the bird. Had it gone to the bottom never to return, I wondered. Was it down there hovering over the molten core of the volcano, silhouetted against the eerie green light?

Clang. Clang. Clang. High on the rim of the crater the Ethiopian cook whacked the iron girder that hung from the dining room eaves. Each clap of this bell came to us a second after the cook struck, sometimes loud, sometimes soft, depending on the gusts of wind.

Mom turned to comment. She had been right: we were late for supper. But when Dad lifted his eyebrows high and cocked his head, she smiled sweetly, and some happy agreement passed between them without words.

I hooted. Johnathan and Nat joined in. Who cared about supper or the lost darter? This was the way life ought to be. We were a family together in the middle of a beautiful lake, a family removed from the whole world, and we were happy.

I could have stayed there, on that lake, all night. I could have slept out there under the stars, with the lap-lapping of the lake on the aluminum sides of our canoe. But when the sun rose again on this paradise of water and wind and fluttering bird life, I couldn't even get near it. We were all locked into the indoor routine that missionaries so carefully observed on Sundays: stiff clothes, somber hymns, a treatise on sanctification.

We met for our church service in the lounge next to the Bishoftu dining hall. After spending Saturday outside, I hated the smell of this closed space, which usually served as a library. My love of stories would have ordinarily drawn me to the shelves of books, but now I recoiled from the musty old-paper odor of all this "appropriate" reading material: Danny Orlis adventures that ended in conversion, crumbling hardbacks about missionaries who nearly died from witch-doctor curses, *Reader's Digest* magazines full of "Drama in Real Life."

I squirmed in my long pants and itchy button-down shirt as the minister droned on like an actor wearied by his script. There was none of the tiptoe, nearly airborne feeling that I had gotten when the burlap bag fell from my shoulders in *Pilgrim's Progress*. I felt heavy instead. We sang "Stand up, stand up for Jesus, ye soldiers of the cross." And when the minister finally bowed his head to close in prayer, I kept my eyes open.

"Give safety, Lord, to all those traveling to the evangelistic crusade in Jimma, and be present especially to those who come bearing the gospel."

I had lowered my head for appearance's sake, but I kicked methodically at the metal legs of the folding chair in front of me. Dad's sturdy thumb and forefinger pinched the nape of my neck, so I stopped. I risked a sideways glance and saw that he had his own eyes shut, so I turned to the picture window instead — that big box of blue sky broken by the wispy green of a pepper tree. Out there, where nature was going on without me, a Malachite Kingfisher had appeared on a bobbing branch.

The tiny bird preened itself, stroking its out-of-proportion orange beak across its azure shoulder. Its cobalt wings opened a second and folded back. Then, without preamble, the bird dropped away, disappearing dartlike, no doubt plummeting toward the lake.

One, two, three, four, I counted. Surely by five, the kingfisher would be over the water hovering, taking aim. By ten it would strike, hitting the lake so hard that it geysered. Then up it would rise, emerging with accelerated wing beats, straining into the sky with a minnow as silver and slippery as mercury, wriggling in its beak.

Dad's thumb and forefinger had gone lax on my neck. Now they tightened. I understood. I closed my eyes. But why couldn't I be out there, I wondered, with my eyes wide open? If God had made such a bright and bold bird, why couldn't my father and mother and Johnathan and Nat and I all be out there, worshiping God with our eyes and our ears, with our very skins? Why couldn't we be trailing the Malachite Kingfisher into the lakeshore reeds and watching as it perched by the weaverbird nests?

After church and lunch, only a few hours remained before we had to get back into the Land Rover and start toward Addis, yet the whole Bishoftu compound was locked in Sabbath. Naps were mandatory. As we raced each other from the dining hall to our cabin, my brothers and I were scolded by an ancient nurse. "Silence," she commanded, poking her wild white hair out of her cabin's screen door and fixing us with a glare full of brimstone.

Mom and Dad insisted that we had to take a nap as well.

"Why? Why? Why?" we begged, until at last Nat fell asleep and Mom took pity.

"All right, you two can go outside," she whispered. "But be quiet. You understand? And stay away from the water."

We understood only too well. She might as well have said, "But don't have any fun."

Johnathan, in his own funk, sat and stared at the lake. I wandered behind our cabin alone with a Tonka truck I had found in the sandbox. Quietly, I carved the ground there, making roadways and purring my muffled engine up the hill. My heart wasn't in it. I knew Mom and Dad were together inside the cabin asleep. Nat too. What I really wanted was for them to come out here and be with me.

I let the yellow truck fall from my fingers and knelt on the clay bank. The hard white sun was high overhead. The whole slope was asleep. The only sound was the wind in the pepper tree next to me, which made a soughing noise. I snapped off some of the fernlike leaves and crushed them in my fingers. I sniffed at the green residue, recoiling from the burn of pepper.

Though I wanted to think of other things, I kept returning to one unavoidable thought: as soon as this nap time ends, we will pack the Land Rover and drive back to boarding school.

. . .

That night at Bingham Academy, after Mrs. Johnson had tucked me into the lower level of my bunk bed, and after she had turned off the lights and faded down the dim cinder-block hall, I listened for a while to the steady breathing of the other boys in their beds, boys who seemed to have become strangers again. I sniffed at the pepper on my fingers and smelled again the sharp residue of Sabbath at Bishoftu. Wind soughing in the trees. The faraway sun, hard and flat. Nothing human in sight but my own hands.

I fell asleep with that scent, and I dreamed . . .

Soldiers were chasing me — all of them in dark green uniforms with tall black boots, all of them with hard helmets that hid their eyes in shadow. They had shot my brothers, my mother too. Only Dad was left, running in front of me. We were forced onto an impossibly high bridge, so high that Sacred Ibises drifted by, silent on their outspread wings. The bridge suddenly broke off in space and we were trapped, unable to flee any farther. The front soldier lifted his machine gun and pointed it toward us. I could taste death in my mouth, oily and rancid, like butter gone bad. Then Dad jerked me into his arms and leapt.

In my dream we fell as if we had dropped into outer space and would fall forever. We fell as if the ground didn't exist. And as we fell, I came out of myself, so that I saw everything like a camera shooting film. There we were, stretched out on our backs with arms and legs spread-eagled. Our sleeves and cuffs whipped in the wind and our hair streamed upward.

Was there water below us? Maybe a lake, like Lake Bishoftu?

If so, would it slow our descent enough for us to survive? Would we lift back out of the water, arms beating like the wings of the Malachite Kingfisher?

Or would the lake plume and swallow us whole, taking us down to its mysterious depths, right down to the green glow of the magma? Would we sink as deep as the African Darter — descending to where the earth's primal heat was bubbling, infernal and ready to erupt?

Riot Drill

AFTER THE BISHOFTU WEEKEND I kept dreaming that same nightmare — about my father and I being chased by soldiers. We always ran out onto that same impossibly high bridge. I knew it would break off, but I was helpless to do anything about it. Dad and I ran single file, muscles cramping, chests burning, until the ground was a vague field of brown half-hidden under clouds. We just kept running, hearing the clump of boots behind us, and the clatter of rifles. Prey and predators. Doomed. But one morning before dawn, something interrupted my dream before I had reached the place where the bridge broke off and Dad lifted me into his arms to leap.

"Timmy. Wake up. Quiet now. Get in line with the others."

Why was Mrs. Johnson leaning over me in the dark, I wondered. For some reason she was waking me in the still of night, when not even the roosters had started to crow. Had something actually happened to my parents? Were they OK?

I rubbed at my eyelids and blinked, trying to understand what she was whispering to my dormmates, and why some of them were standing at the doorway in their PJs.

"OK, everyone get in line," she murmured. But why? And why was no one turning on the lights?

"Quietly now. Down the hallway. No one say a word."

In the dark, we bumped into other confused boys who were also filing out of their rooms. Mr. Johnson was there, arranging us with his big, hairy hands, steering us into a single line. I could barely see the black rectangles of his glasses suspended on his long, pale face. Then we stumbled out the second-story door and moved down the concrete ramp to the parking lot. We shivered in the chill night air, glancing up at the black shell of the sky where it was punctured by a thousand pinprick stars. The silence of the night seemed immense, not to be tampered with by children like us, and accordingly I remained completely quiet, holding my thoughts inside, comforted that at least this wasn't about my parents.

On the cinders of the parking lot, I watched the shadowy figures of older boys and girls moving out of their dorms too. They came down the steps toward us and bent around the lower level of Gowan Hall, snaking toward the wood shop that lay under the dining hall — a garage-sized room full of worktables and electric tools. Silently, mysteriously, they disappeared one by one through the wide, barred doors, until it was our turn and we had entered the dark room.

I couldn't help it. "What's going on?" I whispered. But I got no answer.

Where were all the other children? I wanted to know. Shouldn't there be a whole crowd? But I couldn't see them or feel their body heat or hear anything.

The file kept shuffling forward, as if walking into the back wall. I realized, in fact, that they *were* walking into the wall. I could just make out a section of pegboard swung open on hidden hinges. Screwdrivers and hammers and hacksaws dangled from this secret door. I stepped through the gap and stood in utter blackness, reaching for the shirt of the boy in front of me. It was a damp, earthy place filled with the breathing of children. When I reached to my side, I felt cool clay. The air smelled cold and heavy like the air in the cavelike room where the laundresses did their work.

Why this silence and dark? Was this some kind of religious lesson? Perhaps Jesus' tomb?

A man spoke: "Do we have all the primary grades?"

"First grade, second, and third," Mr. Johnson stage-whispered.

"What about the older kids?"

"We're here too," murmured a woman deep in the darkness. "Both boys and girls."

"Good, then let's see how long it took."

A match burst to life. A blue-and-white flame settled on a wick, and a lamp revealed our principal bending over his wristwatch.

He grimaced, then straightened. "Twelve minutes. Looks like we're going to have to work on it."

In the candlelight I could see the faces of my dormmates now, yellow and uplifted. I could see Danny Coleman gulping nervously, the whites of his eyes showing against his freckled skin. I could see Kenny with his smooth brown skin and white teeth, smiling as if he refused to worry. I could also see Mary Dye with a group of the third-grade girls, her black hair tangled, her large eyes blinking behind heavy glasses.

We were all waiting, equally baffled.

"OK, you can turn on the lights," the principal announced, and there was an explosion of white electric light.

I squinted, and when I could focus, I found that I was in a long, underground tunnel. The ceiling of the tunnel was actually the floorboards of the dining hall, along which a line of light bulbs dangled.

"You're all probably wondering why we brought you down here," the principal said brightly.

"No kidding," some teenager muttered.

"Well, there's a reason. Unfortunately, there has been some trouble in Addis. Nothing you really need to worry about, just some college students who have been stirring up problems."

"What have they been doing?" asked the same boy.

"I'd rather not get into it. I just want everyone to be ready to come down here — if we have to. If a dorm parent tells you to go to the tunnel, or if a teacher tells you, then get down here as quickly as you can."

"Then what?"

The principal ignored him: "And don't tell other people about the tunnel. No one but your parents. Understood?"

So we were hiding after all, and there was something threatening out there. But if the tunnel was supposed to remain a secret just for missionary children and teachers and parents, then what about the laundresses? How could they not know about this place, since it had been dug right next to their workroom? And what about the cook and the dining room staff? Would none of them join us here?

"All right," the principal added. "Soon we're going to have to do another one of these drills, because we weren't fast enough."

"Cool," whispered one of the older kids, and I nudged Danny, trying to get into the spirit of it all. He looked back with a half-smile, still not convinced. I grinned anyway. This was just a drill. It would be fun to do again. Like playing capture the flag after dark — or like a massive hide-and-seek. It would be a giant game.

I could see my brother Johnathan not far away with a cluster of his sixth-grade friends, his kinked brown hair askew from lying on his pillow. I lifted my thumb and, instead of ignoring me, he lifted his thumb in agreement.

Then the principal called for attention. "Before we all go back to bed, I have one more thing to add: what about a snack?"

Applause rang out, and the principal beamed, his sandy hair glistening in the overhead light, his face turned remarkably genial. The dorm parents began handing trays over our heads, along with stacks of plastic glasses.

"Everyone gets just two cookies, and one glass of Kool-Aid."

Someone's head bumped a light bulb and it swung, making our shadows lurch and dance. We nibbled our cookies in the swaying light, all of us in bathrobes and flip-flops. We partied in little bunches, first-graders and sixth-graders and ninth-graders, licking our red, Kool-Aid-stained lips, half awake, half asleep, not sure whether any of this was real.

As I sipped from my own green plastic cup and exchanged gibes with my classmates, I remained sleepily semiconscious. A thought flickered in my barely alert mind, that somewhere out there in the gaping blackness, a gang of young men might be gathering and taking to the streets. Then the thought was gone, shoved back into the dim recesses of my mind, along with other abandoned ideas. I packed it away: a remote shout, a faraway staccato of sticks whacking tin, the *shush* of glass shattering. I chose to be unconcerned, instead, standing in that weird corridor with my peers.

The sky was turning pale when we exited and returned to the dorms. No doubt by then our laundresses were awake, starting to cook food for their families or already wrapping their shawls over their shoulders in preparation for the long walk to the academy. No doubt the cooks were also on their way to prepare our breakfast. What was it like for them to hike the long miles in the morning chill, leaving their own children to care for us? I didn't know and I didn't really want to think about it. I was too happy whispering to Danny Coleman as we went up the ramp into our dorm. If riots meant more adventure like this, then bring them on.

Besieged

AS MAY GAVE WAY to June and July, the light rains came and went. The heavy rains took hold — unloosing over Addis Ababa every afternoon and cascading down in sheets, until one afternoon the torrent turned hard and clattered on the roofs. Hail fell for thirty minutes, turning the soccer pitch white. We ran out and popped the icy marbles into our mouths. We packed them into hail balls and thwacked each other.

With the rains came the hope of home. I allowed myself to consider returning to my parents and Nat, this time for a two-month vacation. I felt proud to have survived my first year at Bingham Academy. I was no longer one of the kids who didn't know how things worked.

Dad flew up alone to fetch Johnathan and me, and since we couldn't afford to fly back, the three of us made a harrowing trip to Leimo aboard a top-heavy bus. The sullen driver seemed bent on killing any animal that lingered on the gravel. He ran over a goat, which flopped on the shoulder of the road like a beached fish. He even took down a donkey, not braking or swerving, just thunking its hips off the road.

I felt sad for these animals, but I wasn't too afraid because I was with my father and older brother. When we stopped in the valley across from Leimo station and I saw Mom and Nat running up the dirt road from the stream, I quit hanging onto the aluminum rim of the window and pushed my way down the aisle. I came off the bus like a veteran home from the front.

At Leimo, I celebrated my new freedom, waking eagerly every morning and galloping everywhere. The rains didn't keep me or my brothers from playing outside. We ran out into the puddles and rivulets, making boats from folded paper or even better ones from cut plywood, with rubber-band motors that spun plywood paddles.

Johnathan also organized Nat and me and the four Dye kids (my old girlfriend, Mary, her brother, Mark, and two sisters, Ruthie and Cathy) into Olympic teams, getting permission for us to create official competitors' shirts by drawing our names with black marker on white T-shirts. We erected pole-vaulting standards and hurdles of bamboo stakes with tied crossbars. We even ran the steeple-chase, riding poles as our horses.

Local children gathered on the perimeter of our Olympic field and leaned on their walking sticks shepherd-style, whispering as we passed. We ignored them, except for Nat, who had gotten to know a few of the younger ones in our absence and acknowledged them with a quick nod. "That's Sawo," he said. "The one with the blue shirt."

Sawo smiled back, but we just nodded and went on with our plans, not sure how to include this younger child without opening the competition to older kids, all of whom looked remarkably lean and wiry and, no doubt, fast. So we played in a separate realm, tied to something we had only heard about: the distant glory of athletes competing at a world level.

The legendary Ethiopian runner Abebe Bikila had just competed at the 1968 Mexico Olympics, trying to add another medal to the two golds he had won in the past, first at Rome (where he ran barefoot on cobblestones), then at Tokyo (where he won despite recent appendicitis). Bikila had *not* won at Mexico City. However, he was returning to Ethiopia as an established legend — a peasant boy who had become the first runner ever to win consecutive

Olympic marathons. He was Johnathan's hero and a good bit of the inspiration for our games. After Johnathan told us about Bikila's epic accomplishments, we all wanted to be just as fast and tough, even though, ironically, all our Hadiya neighbors were forced to stand off to the side watching as we tried to emulate their fellow countryman.

Nat was the only one who actually played with the local kids. When Johnathan and I had no energy to continue, he and several of the youngest ones ran their own sprints, taking turns holding a white string for the finish line. They also pushed each other on Nat's tricycle, going in tight circles until the vehicle toppled out of control. However, as soon as Nat saw us starting some new activity, he broke away from Sawo and his gang, waving to make sure they understood that he was leaving. Once again he would play apart from the local children — in a Western world with his *ferengi* brothers.

This state of affairs continued until one afternoon, in the middle of an imagined Olympic pole vault, an adult broke through the invisible barrier we had been keeping between us and the outer world. We had set up a landing pit with a heap of cut grass and sawdust. We were taking turns running at the crossbar and flinging ourselves over when an *ibbed* woman came dashing pell-mell onto our compound.

Ibbed meant insane, and we knew that *ibbed* people did crazy things, just like the crazy man who had kicked at Nat on the DC-3, making it impossible to say a proper goodbye to Mom and Dad. Such people wandered freely, since there was no place to put them. We and the Dye kids had all seen them before, sometimes muttering and twisting their heads as if tormented by gnats. But we had never seen an *ibbed* person as wild as this one. She came sprinting, bare-chested, with her long, pointy breasts flapping. She screamed and lectured at everything she saw — the hospital, the tree house we had built, the pet goat on the grass. Then she ran into the sheets that Mom had hung to dry. One sheet tore loose, and she galloped for the hills still wrapped in this white cloth, so that we could see her a mile away tumbling along like a piece of paper on the wind.

Terrified by this woman's antics, we scattered. When we came back together, we joked nervously. We tried to return to our imaginative routine, but her intrusion had left a permanent chill, as if she were the messenger of worse things to come. And perhaps she was a harbinger, for not long after her mad dash bigger trouble *did* emerge. Two other mission families unexpectedly arrived from Hosanna station, near the town where the bus had dropped us off at the beginning of the vacation, and from the beginning it was clear that the other missionaries were fleeing some major difficulty at Hosanna.

I could tell that the two families were vulnerable, not so much because of anything they did or said, but because of how cheerful and solicitous everyone else seemed when around them. One family, the Stinsons, moved into a tent in our yard. The other family, the Esterlines, moved into our storage shed. And as Mr. Dye worked enthusiastically on converting the storage shed into a temporary home, I began to wonder in earnest. I tagged along as he helped Mr. Esterline roll barrels of gasoline out of the space and stack crates of canned goods in a corner. They put up army cots and tarred the roof as if this arrangement was going to last longer than a few days. And then, since they had no kitchen, Mrs. Esterline came over to our house to cook a meal. So did Mrs. Stinson. Soon they were in and out of our house every day, cooking and eating and washing dishes.

"When are the other families going to go home?" I asked Mom and Dad after a week, but I got only evasive answers.

"Soon," they said. "They just need some time away, that's all."

"But why did they have to get away?"

"It's too complicated to explain. Don't worry. They'll only be here for a few more weeks."

When Mom was diagnosed with hepatitis and couldn't cook anymore, the shared kitchen arrangement proved beneficial. For a month Mom was supposed to stay in bed and read books. Doctor's orders—Dad's orders, to be precise. So Mrs. Esterline and Mrs. Stinson took turns cooking for our family as well. While they did, Johnathan, Nat, and I got out of the way and lolled on Mom's bed as she read aloud from C. S. Lewis's *Chronicles of Narnia,* taking us off to an imaginary land where knights held court with talking animals and dwarfs.

Something must have really gone wrong in Hosanna, because nobody would explain it. My brothers and I remained in the dark until one morning, after several weeks, Dad said we would take a day trip to the other station. He hoisted us into the back of the Land Rover, plunking us down on the firm side benches. Mr. and Mrs. Stinson climbed into the front cab with him, and off we went.

Ever since we had gotten stuck in the river three years ago on the way to the Bolosso station, I had relished Land Rover trips. Any road trip was a potential adventure, so I was happy to be included. I bounced next to Johnathan and reached for the ceiling. Nat bounced in imitation. However, when we arrived at the Hosanna station, all three of us grew still instantly. The moment we entered the gates, we could see that the compound was absolutely vacant, as if the rapture had occurred and everyone had been taken up to heaven.

We shut our mouths and stared as the Land Rover puttered down the tree-lined center lane. When we got out, we just stood around as cats will do in a strange place—all three of us scanning the territory, sniffing the strange air, and taking single cautious steps.

To stand inside that well-established, fenced compound—with all the silent flowering shrubs and the leafy paths and the dark, sleepy houses—was to know immediately that something sinister was afoot. This was obviously a place for people to gather, so where were the Ethiopian women on the doorsteps selling eggs, or the children peeking from behind houses to spy on the white *ferengis?* Where were the workers squatting in the grass with sickles, or the teenagers who should be reciting answers under the tin roof of the school building?

Mr. Stinson unlocked the front door of a house, and we followed closely into the shadows. Inside, I noticed one broken window, then another. That was not right. Birds might fly in, or mosquitoes.

Dad murmured quietly to Mr. and Mrs. Stinson, and the house echoed their soft sounds. Now and then, they looked out the front window as if anticipating something. Dad stooped and picked an object off the wooden floor. It was a rock the size of an egg.

They all spread out, walking from room to room, taking their own inventories. Mrs. Stinson selected a few books off the shelves and rummaged in a cabinet for kitchen utensils. Mr. Stinson got tools out of a cupboard. Dad cleaned glass off the floor and put it in a metal trash basket. He seemed nervous and tentative, like a burglar who had stayed too long.

"C'mon, boys," Dad called out, ushering us toward the front door.

"Hey, a swing," I yelled, and began racing toward the dangling seat with Nat in pursuit.

"Not now!" Dad barked.

"But why?"

"Boys!" Dad called out, his voice tight. "Into the Land Rover! I'm going to count to three."

"Aw, Dad," we chorused, but we knew better than to ignore him. We slumped back to the vehicle, where Johnathan was already waiting.

What a strange trip. Why drive so far just to stop for a few minutes? There were so many good climbing trees. And wasn't that a whole trellis of passion fruit, ripe and ready?

"Dad, can we just stop and pick a few passion fruit?" I begged. I could taste the tart juice, but Dad didn't answer as he kept us rolling toward the station gate. In fact, no one spoke much all the way back to Leimo. The adults stayed quiet, and we stayed quiet too, hoping to catch some accidental clue to the whole situation.

It wasn't until that night, after prayers, that Johnathan had the nerve to ask the question I had been forming all afternoon: "Dad, how come everyone had to leave the Hosanna station?"

"J.B., it's too late. The lights are off."

"But how come?"

"Some kids got carried away. That's all. And they did some stupid things."

"What sort of stuff?"

Wanting to get in on the conversation, I chipped in, "Did they bust the windows?"

Dad sighed heavily. "Boys . . . go to sleep."

"Do you think they might come here?" I blurted out.

"No! It's not something you have to worry about. In a few weeks the Stinsons and the Esterlines should be back at Hosanna and everything will be back to normal."

"But why did the kids do those things?"

Mom jumped in, trying to get it all squared away. "It wasn't really their fault. Some new teachers had come from Addis Ababa. Young people from the college there. And they were the ones who started it all."

Were these rabble-rousers the same college students who had been causing trouble in Addis a few months ago? Johnathan must have had the same thought, because he told Mom and Dad about the riot drill. They seemed genuinely surprised. It was news to them. They peered at each other in the semidark of the room, their silhouettes outlined by the lamp glow from the next room.

"In fact, those probably were some of the same people," said Mom. "A few months ago they caused so much trouble in Addis that the Emperor closed the college and told them they all had to serve as teachers in the country. He said that if they wanted reform in Ethiopia, they could help make the changes."

"Doesn't sound like it worked too well," whispered Johnathan.

"No, it sure doesn't," said Dad, staring out the bedroom window toward the black sky and the tiny sparks of light so far away. "I don't think this is what he had in mind."

Hidden Agendas

BEFORE WE HAD COME HOME on holiday, Mom and Dad had bought Nat two pet goats, one light and one dark — Salt and Pepper. We gave them attention now and then, like we had given attention to our pet *madoqua* at Soddo. While we patted their bristly backs, they dropped their heads against our thighs, pushing with their knobby skulls as if trying to reposition us. I straddled them and lowered my weight onto their backs, which made Nat protest. He needn't have worried, since the goats always backed out from under me and scampered away.

Most of the time, Salt and Pepper just grazed their way across the yard, cropping grass alongside Johnathan's horse, Gillian, then chewing studiously. It was a surprise when Dad announced that he needed to borrow one of them for medical purposes. Nat, who was very softhearted, said no. He didn't want the goat to be hurt.

Dad explained that if he could practice this particular operation — which had something to do with intestines — then he might be able to save the life of a patient. He said that the goat should be fine when it was all done.

Nat, who was now worried about the welfare of the patient, said, "OK, but be careful."

Unfortunately, Pepper didn't survive. The anesthesia mask didn't fit and Dad overcompensated, accidentally overdosing the goat on ether. That meant he had to try again — this time with Salt. Nat was devastated, but Dad went ahead anyway. He succeeded with Salt, and the gray goat returned to our yard, groggy but standing.

Something had changed, however. Now that Salt was the only goat left, he seemed pathetic and therefore less interesting. Dad tried to cheer Nat by depicting Salt as a medical hero. He announced that the operation on the man with intestinal problems had been a success, all due to Salt the Wonder Goat. But neither Nat nor Johnathan nor I showed the same attention to the orphaned goat that we had shown to the pair.

With the end of the crisis at Hosanna station, the Stinsons and the Esterlines moved out of their temporary shelters and returned to their homes. At night we put Salt in the vacated shed because the hyenas were coming close again. But now even the hyenas seemed routine. As the holiday extended and we used up any remaining playing ideas, we lay around the house, complaining that there was nothing to do. Mom told us to help pick lettuce from the garden, or help wash dishes, or sweep the kitchen floor, but we burst out in indignation, knowing that she was baiting us. That is, until one day she offered a more intriguing alternative. It was still quite practical, but it was a hundred times more interesting than gardening or sweeping, and that is because it involved money. Mom suggested that we organize a fundraiser for the hospital. She said that maybe we could gather enough money to buy the new microscope Dad needed for the pathology department, where the dressers were being trained to check stools for parasites.

All we needed was something to sell, and Mom had the perfect idea — tin cans. Here in the Leimo area, tin cans were a commodity. The only containers owned by the local people were clay pots, which took lots of time to make, cost quite a bit, and were easily broken. A sturdy can, guaranteed to bounce if it fell, would be a useful addition in any Hadiya home.

So we went to work, running to the Dyes's house to get their kids involved, then running to Nurse Marie and Nurse Chris for their cans, and then to the hospital for more. We gathered thirty or forty of these unlikely treasures, all of which had been brought to Leimo by Land Rover with supply shipments from Addis. In our hands they received new value. We tore away their labels and scrubbed their stained insides to a bright sheen. On the appointed day, we arranged our wares in rows on a card table next to the hospital entrance, as if we were opening a stall in the Hosanna marketplace. Tuna cans were the smallest and least expensive, a nickel apiece. Then there were the midsize fruit cans that held peaches or pears, worth closer to a dime. Best of all was a stack of coffee cans, which local women coveted for their size and all-around usefulness. These we priced at the equivalent of an Ethiopian quarter.

All day, local women came hiking up the muddy wheel ruts from the stream, barefoot and perspiring. They fingered the cans, examining them like glass mixing bowls at a department store. They haggled with us, aiming for a slightly lower price, and when we gave in, they untied their cloth belts and unwrapped the few precious coins they had brought.

As the day stretched on, we counted and recounted our coins, wonderful heavy copper coins stamped with the Emperor's face, high forehead and all. The solid weight of the money made us feel important. We were delighted that we could take such throwaway articles — pure junk — and turn them into profit. The only cans I would have used myself were the coffee cans that Mom kept in our bedroom closet so that we could pee in them at night when we were afraid to go to the outhouse. And look at this: similar cans were bringing in twenty-five cents apiece, adding up eventually to whole Ethiopian *birr*.

We smiled and tolerated the touch of these peasant women, many of whom wanted to feel our straight hair, especially Nat's bright yellow hair. We interacted with them as we never had done before, attempting to negotiate in Amharic, trying out Hadiya phrases that were new to us, even resorting to pantomimes. We struck hard deals, and after we had turned over the five Ethiopian *birr* we had raised to help buy the microscope, we felt righteously satisfied, pleased by our own Christian industry and charity. We had contributed to the cause. We had helped with the central work of the Leimo station — the hospital.

During that vacation, I came to the hospital whenever allowed. I often asked to come with Dad on his morning rounds, knowing that the Ethiopian dressers would greet me by name and quiz me in their broken English. Yonas was still there, along with several others from Wolaita, and they liked to talk to me about the Soddo hospital and Dr. Barlow. But even the Hadiya and Kambattan dressers spoke enough English to engage me in a simple conversation.

Dad was comfortable with these fellow staff, who seemed to brighten when they saw him. He responded to them in the national language, Amharic, making them smile. He asked them about their children and relatives.

I followed Dad into the patient wards too, where patients and their families greeted him with deference, bowing slightly. He would engage them with a Hadiya greeting — *Ttuma* — which brought smiles and a greater level of ease. Then he would switch over into Amharic or turn to a dresser for translation. The patients who had stayed for more than a few days, at least those who were recovering, tended to smile when they saw Dad. Many called out to him. However, there were other patients with pulled-down brows and wrinkles between their eyebrows. These patients stayed silent and looked at everyone askance: Dad, the dressers, Nurse Marie. If Dad tried to introduce me from where I stood at the foot of their beds, they scowled.

Whole families came into the hospital with these sour expressions, and some left the same way. They argued on their way out, refusing to pay the minimal prices, saying that the medicine or the surgery wasn't worth that much. They haggled with the hospital accountant, demanding to speak with the doctor in charge. Then they narrowed their eyes and shook their heads if Dad tried to explain how costs had been lowered, subsidized by the mission. They didn't believe that all this medical care was being offered at much less than what it cost. And often they got away with paying less, even though Nurse Marie protested and said that it was flat wrong to give in to them.

Some days Dad grimaced during dinner, as if the food were giving him pain. He confided in Mom about the more resistant patients, or their families. He said one father had taken his daughter out of her bed and carried her away, even though he'd been told that she would die without surgery. The man said that a girl was not worth that much money. Dad sensed that other patients didn't trust the treatments he prescribed. They had come because they were desperate, but they acted as if all these scientific approaches — pills, shots, casts, surgeries — were no better than the potions and incantations and sacrifices of their traditional healers. He was sure that a witch doctor was out there, maybe several of them, standing against the mission. One of the dressers had said as much.

It was stressful for Dad to treat people, knowing that they didn't trust him. He wanted to get it right so that there would be less skepticism. But to compound the problem, there was Nurse Marie standing in the shadows, always watching, unimpressed. Whenever Marie was in the same room with Dad, he became sober and quiet, unlike the way he was with the dressers or with Nurse Chris or Mrs. Dye when she was on duty. Marie and Dad spoke in short, terse sentences, avoiding each other's eyes.

One evening after supper, while Dad was watching Mom wash the dishes, he said that he wished he had a way to unite the staff more. "They need clearer guidelines, especially about how to treat patients."

She said, "Well, why don't you type up some objectives? You could post them in the hospital. It would give you an excuse to meet and talk."

"You know who wouldn't like that."

"Marie?" I asked.

I had spoken up from the table, where I was still working on a mound of mashed potatoes, picking out the clumps that hadn't gotten mashed. Mom raised one of her eyebrows. "Tim, you need to finish up and go on out with your brothers."

"But I want to know who it is."

"That's not something you need to know. Plate in the sink."

So I went outside to find my brothers. In the little light that was left, Johnathan was chopping a log into L-shaped steps. It was going to be our Jacob's ladder, for climbing into the tree house. Nat was happy just to watch the notches appear, but I wanted to participate and Johnathan wouldn't relinquish the hatchet. Bored, I slipped back into the living room, where I eavesdropped from the couch. Dad was dictating as Mom typed. He had just finished a sentence that ended with the words *ministering in Christ's name.*

The typewriter clacked to a stop. Then Dad said, "If people reject us, they will reject our message. Period."

The typewriter clacked to a stop again, and he said, "You know, I probably need to have something about finances too."

"All right."

He paused, then spoke it off in slow measured phrases: "Our responsibility is to treat the sick. Period. This takes precedence over financial considerations. Period." He let Mom catch up, then went on, "Where finances take precedence over this, we are running contrary to the spirit of the New Testament. Period."

While the typewriter was still clattering, he said, "She's going to protest. You know she will. I'd better have a verse."

"You could use the verse about helping widows and orphans."

"Maybe, but isn't there one in Acts that uses the word *poor.* Something like 'remember the poor . . .' "

I could hear the rustling of tissuey pages, the sort found in a Bible. "What chapter do you think it's in?" Mom asked.

"Maybe 19 or 20?"

"Remember the poor, support the weak . . ."

"That's it. That's perfect."

I could hear Mom's typewriter clacking again.

"I'm going to need something about attitudes on the job too."

"All right."

"Our job ... no, scratch that. How about 'Work here at Leimo ...'"

The typewriter sprang into action again, clapping and ringing. "Work here at Leimo, despite the constant presence of sorrow and suffering, should have an element of joy. Period. It should have a sense of privilege. Comma. A spirit of adventure. Comma. An attitude of quest. Comma. Invention. Comma. Innovation. Period."

He went on, caught up in the stream of oratory: "Underdeveloped countries are just finding their way as to how health needs can best be met. Period. We should entertain an attitude of privilege to even be here. Period. We have a responsibility. Comma. To both workers and patients. Comma. To educate. Period. The attitude with which we view those we minister to is very important. Period. Are they ignorant or unteachable. Question mark. Or have we really tried to teach. Question mark."

The typewriter dinged and clicked to a stop. Then Dad exhaled as if he had lifted a heavy weight. "She's going to think it's directed at her, but it's not just about her. I mean, some of the dressers lord it over the patients too. They've got the same attitude. But you know Marie; she's going to think I wrote it just for her."

I sat up now because I had gotten my answer. I was right. Once again Marie was the one Dad was up against.

"Charles, maybe she just needs to hear it coming straight from you. You've been wanting to say these things for months. Better this way than in an argument."

"Then I better tackle the real problem."

"What do you mean?"

"It's about who's in charge. That's what it boils down to. So shouldn't I add a section on leadership?"

Mom was in support mode. "Why not? You can always cut it if you decide it's too much."

Dad took a big breath. I could almost feel a vacuum. Then he started dictating again: "It is understood that the mission council — let's capitalize both words — has gone on record stating that the doctor is the head of the hospital. Period. Therefore it is the doctor's responsibility to put before the staff the policies and practices of the hospital. Period. It is the responsibility of the staff to adhere to these policies . . ." and here he paused, before continuing "unless for moral or other reasons the staff cannot adhere to them. Period. If a staff member cannot subscribe to these policies. Comma. Then to not jeopardize that individual's conscience and for the need of being of one mind. Comma. That person should seek reappointment to a situation to which they can comply."

Before the typewriter had stopped clacking, Dad had asked Mom, "So what do you think?"

"I think it's honest but fair. I think it takes pains to allow for the other person's point of view. I think you should keep it."

I had risen from the couch and moved to the doorway. I felt guilty for eavesdropping but also excited about figuring out what was going on. Now I poked my head into the kitchen and said, "I think it's good too, Dad!"

They both swiveled, startled, as if they had been caught standing in someone else's house.

"Young man, how long have you been listening?" Mom asked.

"Johnathan wouldn't let me use the hatchet."

"How long?"

"Just a while."

They both stared at me.

"Well, this is not something for you to repeat. Do you understand?"

"Yes . . . but I think you should use it, even if Marie doesn't agree."

They were amused. Dad lifted his brows as if surprised by my advice. "Are you sure about that?"

When I nodded, then he nodded too. "Well, then, maybe that's just what we'll do."

There were a few Christians around Leimo whose faith dated back as far as Ato Wandaro, the church founder who had created such an inspiration in Soddo by refusing to recant during the

Italian occupation. The missionaries who had journeyed into the Soddo area in 1927 had come to Leimo first, and the church had slowly taken root since then. However, the Hadiya and Kambattan churches had never shown the same sweeping energy as in Soddo and the Wolaita district. While hundreds of Wolaitans had asked to be baptized again this year during the annual evangelism crusade, Kambattan and Hadiya schoolchildren had rioted against the mission. While the Soddo mission hospital was growing tremendously, the Leimo hospital was struggling to establish itself, with some patients completely refusing to pay for treatment. Whenever Mom and Dad spoke about the church in Soddo, they became wistful, impressed by the generosity and commitment of the Christians there. But they sighed when talking about the Hadiya and Kambattan people. Why was everyone so resistant?

Nevertheless, the local church did have its core of faithful leaders, and one of those leaders whom my parents respected greatly was a man named Ato Aba Goli. Unlike gentle Wandaro with his lean body and gap-toothed smile, Ato Aba Goli was a thickset, powerful man whose torso loomed above his legs, looking top-heavy after he had wrapped his *shamma* around his neck. He laughed big, walked big, and spoke so loudly that he could be heard two rooms away.

When he rode his mule, Ato Aba Goli made the animal seem small, standing high on the stirrups with his toes nearly grazing the short bunch grass. He was nothing like Ato Wandaro. He had such a commanding presence that he took charge of nearly every conversation. On the other hand, he took great pleasure in laughter. My father became jovial around Ato Aba Goli. They were both big, solid men who appreciated a joke.

Soon after Dad had composed the new hospital objectives, we were invited to Ato Aba Goli's church, and as we rode there, Dad kept up a lively conversation with Ato Aba Goli. Johnathan and I were on our gelding, Gillian. Mom was riding a rented mule, and Dad and Nat were sharing a rented mule. But Ato Aba Goli led the way on his favorite steed, a quick-footed white mule. As we forded a stream, he teased Johnathan and me about crocodiles, telling us they were partial to horse meat. He also told us to lift our feet high, just in case.

After church, Ato Aba Goli demanded that we stay and eat, refusing my parents' attempt not to burden him. We waited another two hours as the food was cooked, nibbling on parched corn as his daughter roasted coffee beans over the open fire and ground them up and brewed coffee for Mom and Dad, so that the one-room house grew thick with the rich scent. Then his wife starting laying out the *injera* and the *wat*.

It was a feast. There were ladles of *doro wat* and *alitcha wat* and *ʒiguni wat*, poured out on spread *injera*. And his wife brought each of us several more rolls of *injera* like rolled-up napkins. She popped the caps off warm Fantas, and Ato Aba Goli commanded us to eat and eat and eat, until we could hardly bring our hands to our mouths.

In honor of my father's friendship, the evangelist tore off a big scrap of *injera* and dipped it deep in the *ʒiguni wat*, wrapping a bundle of the spicy meat until it was the size of a small potato. Then he told Dad to open his mouth, and he stuffed it in, laughing. "*Goursha*," he called it, telling us that this was the custom for true friends.

Ato Aba Goli was in high form as he escorted us home that afternoon, insisting that it was no problem really — "*Gidelem, minim idelem*." He began to tease Johnathan as we were working our way downhill through a large eucalyptus forest. He wanted to know whether Gillian could run.

"Of course he can."

"I don't know. He looks very tired."

"He's fine. He's just taking it easy. He's actually a racer."

"A horse that can race? I don't think so — not like a mule."

"Oh, c'mon," Johnathan replied, seeing now where this was headed. "Gillian could beat any mule. Everyone knows that mules are slow."

The challenge had been extended and now the race was set. I

slipped down off Gillian's rump and climbed up behind Mom. The two competitors reined in their steeds, side by side, waiting between two trees. Then, on Dad's command, they kicked the animals and shouted them into action.

From the start, it was apparent that Gillian was in trouble. While he shied and skittered down the slope, nervously swinging around obstacles, the little white mule went into a confident trot, becoming a four-legged swivel that switched back and forth without pause. Gillian was two horses — a front and back in disagreement. The mule was a single unit of motion.

They disappeared into the forest, and we followed at a trot. Finally, at the bottom of the hill where the forest gave way to a farmer's field, we found the racers waiting. Gillian was panting, head down. The mule, by contrast, tossed its head and champed at the bit. As for Ato Aba Goli? He had a very satisfied smile on his face.

His voice boomed: "Char-less, you must ask your son which one of us was the winner?"

"So who was it?" Dad asked.

"Ato Aba Goli," Johnathan muttered. "But no fair. I bet Gillian could win on a field."

"Ar-ra you sure? Should we try maybe?" Ato Aba Goli asked.

"No way. You know he's too tired."

He laughed. "Then you must agree, I think, that my mule is the fastest? *Hylenya*, no?"

"All right. I agree she is the *hylenya* one. At least for today."

Ato Aba Goli laughed again, one of his deep belly laughs, holding his reins high as the mule circled in a standing trot.

That was a fun Sunday outing for us all, and Dad was relaxed right through breakfast time the next morning. However, Monday evening at supper he grimaced again, as if each bite brought him pain. Johnathan and Nat cleared their places and ran outside. I went to the living room with a set of colored chalks, intending to draw and color a cathedral that I had found on a Christmas card that Mom had kept in one of our photo albums. My parents were silent in the kitchen, except for the occasional splash of dishwater. Then Mom asked quietly, "Charles?"

After a moment she added, "Something's bothering you, but I can't know if you don't tell me."

He blew out softly. "Same old story. Marie and I. Only this time she said that maybe I ought to go back to the States. She thinks I don't really belong on the mission field."

Mom sighed. "If only she knew. She has no idea, Charles. You can't listen to her when she's like that. It's not true."

"I don't know whether it's true or not. Sometimes I don't even care." And then his chair scraped back.

I pulled my paper and chalk down onto the floor in front of the couch, lying flat so that I would be less noticeable. I couldn't tell whether Dad saw me as he walked out of the kitchen and turned down the hall. But he didn't pause at all. He went right to the bedroom, where he closed the door quietly.

The house was entirely quiet. Even the splashing in the sink had stopped. While it stayed so quiet, I didn't move because I knew that Mom was still in there, listening, waiting, wondering.

Pigeon Fever

JOHNATHAN AND I RETURNED to Bingham Academy in September, and this time I didn't cry. I knew how the routine worked. The Johnsons were still my dorm parents, and I knew what I could expect from them. If I fell on the soccer pitch and tore the scab on my knee, I could expect hydrogen peroxide, not comfort. Also, if I got caught standing in my PJs in the middle of the dorm room, whacking Dave Iwan with a pillow, I could expect fair and impartial punishment — only three to five strikes with the leather strap, no more.

The only real change was that we had a new teacher, Miss Willey. She was the woman who had prepared us for *Pilgrim's Progress,* and I still liked her for her enthusiastic, husky voice. She began each day as if it might hold a surprise. Other than that, everything seemed quite familiar, and there was a kind of security in knowing what to expect each day. Our schedule offered the predictability of ritual.

Evenings could be hard, though, because without distraction I tended to brood. The nightly story time was a reliable relief from my worries. During second grade, we had been read *Little House on the Prairie* and other books by Laura Ingalls Wilder. While listening, I had drifted away into another time and place, out there on the plains where a pioneer girl lived with her family, braving wolves and wildfires and wary Indians. Wilder's stories not only took me out of Bingham Academy but out of my own skin.

Now, instead, Mrs. Johnson began reading from a book by an English missionary named Patricia St. John. *The Tanglewoods' Secret* was a novel about two missionary children who had been left in England with their aunt while their parents worked in India. They were not happy. They roamed in the woods until they met a Gypsy boy. He took them climbing, and one day he climbed higher than he should, up where the whole tree bent in the wind and branches sagged. While this boy was waving down at his friends, a branch snapped, and he came crashing through the lower limbs until he landed flat on his back and lay still.

I had enjoyed the adventures Wilder had had out on the Kansas prairie, but I was not so sure about these two missionary children in England. They seemed too much like me. They had to deal with their parents being away, doing "God's work." And now that the Gypsy boy had died, they were left with all sorts of disturbing worries.

I couldn't sleep after Mrs. Johnson read the chapter about the tree-climbing incident. My old feeling of being lost crept back as I lay in the dark—as if no one knew where I was, not even me. I prayed and prayed, hoping that God was in the room listening. I wanted God to make sure Mom and Dad and Nat were fine back at Leimo. I wanted God to make sure I was fine too. And I hoped God could take care of such things because that was how it was supposed to work, according to the old sheepherder in *The Tanglewoods' Secret*, who had all sorts of wise things to say about Jesus the Good Shepherd.

It was not long after Mrs. Johnson read about the Gypsy boy's death that I began to get fevers. I would recover for a day or two, then run another fever. Mrs. Johnson shook her head after studying the thermometer. "One-hundred and three degrees," she said. "How do you do that?"

She put me in bed, and there I stayed, trying to distract myself with plastic army men. I arranged them all over the crumpled blankets, hiding them in the folds and sending them out to battle. I threw marbles at them like cannon balls. But the next afternoon, when the fever hadn't broken, I began to see strange things. My hands grew to twenty times their normal size with fingers the size of small logs, fingers so heavy that I couldn't lift them. When I did get them into the air, I was afraid they would fall on me and crush me. I put them down by my sides and watched them warily.

My temperature lowered at last, and Mrs. Johnson let me go back to school, but after classes, I didn't feel up to playing. Danny came into the dorm room and found me on the bed reading. "What d'ya wanna do?"

"I don't know."

"We could play soccer."

"Nah, I don't really want to. I think I'll just read."

He stared at me a while, then drifted away. I kept reading until I had finished the whole book — a blue hardback biography of President Andrew Jackson, who had almost gotten his arm cut off during the Revolutionary War because, even though he was only fourteen years old, he refused to clean the boots of a British officer. I lay on my bed thinking how brave Jackson had been and wondering if I could ever have that kind of courage. Then I wandered down the empty hall and out the ramp to the parking lot. I turned toward the cedar forest by the school entrance, stooped under the low-hanging canopy, found a tree with branches I could reach, and began to climb.

This became a habit for me. I returned regularly to the cedar forest and climbed as high as I dared, staying up there above the boarding school to watch as other kids raced around on the cinder driveway near the entrance or staff members chatted or the *zebunya* walked his rounds with his cudgel. My favorite tree was right next to the entrance. When I reached the top of that cedar, the prickly foliage hid me so well that no one could spot me. Up there, I could see over the tin-covered fence to the entrance road. I watched Fiat lorries rumbling by on their way north out of Addis and peasants clambering off overloaded buses to disappear down paths in the forest. Boys my age zigzagged out of the woods, clucking at herds of goats. Men stopped to pee against the fence. Women murmured on the leaf-covered paths, adjusting the bundles of sticks strapped to their backs. And none of these passersby saw me, perched bird-like above their heads.

A light wind rustled the evergreen needles, making the tree whisper and creak and sway side to side. I felt the cool air inside my shirtsleeves, caressing my armpits and chest. It seemed to pass right through me. I was hollowed out, empty, but not unhappy and not afraid. What if I let go? What would happen then?

Nailed to one of the branches of this particular cedar, I found a tuna can with a little offering of dried wheat. The kernels of grain must have been placed there by some older boy who came and went like myself. I suspected that he had put it there for the pigeons that roosted in the hidden recesses of the cedar forest. Maybe he hoped he could tame one and make it his pet.

I wasn't old enough yet to have such a pet, but lots of the bigger boys at Bingham had their own pigeons, which they kept in the large, walk-in cage that was strapped to the lattice of eucalyptus poles along the east wall of the gymnasium. When I walked by, that whole wall cooed and fluttered, as if it might take off and leave the gym. I loved to watch as other boys slipped inside to lift their pigeons out of boxed perches and to feed them. Sometimes they chewed the grain and spat it right into the birds' beaks.

As I listened to the wind riffle through the cedar, I pinched the hard little kernels of grain between my fingers and rolled them clean. Then I chewed on them, enjoying the fermented, gritty taste. I could see for miles — all the way to the peaks of distant hills. Sometimes I imagined that Mom and Dad might surprise me, arriving in the next vehicle that turned up the drive. I waited, watching closely if I heard an engine approach.

When the fever hit again, I was once more restricted to my bed, and this time the school nurse, Mrs. Mead, decided to take my blood. She set up a microscope and a box of glass plates on my dresser, breathing audibly, the way that heavy people do. As I stood next to her, she placed her hand over my palm and pinned it to the dresser. She held a lancet over my index finger, squeezed it between her own thick fingers, then jabbed.

A drop of blood, rose red, swelled into a globe on my fingertip. It shone there and shook. However, as Mrs. Mead searched for her glass microscope plate, her elbow brushed it away.

She breathed heavily, squeezing my finger until it turned purple, but no more blood came.

"All right, we'll have to do it again," she said. And she got another lancet.

Picking a different finger, she pricked me again and transferred the blood onto a glass plate. Only this time she fumbled the slip cover used to seal the lab sample. When she finally got a clean one out of the box, the blood had congealed.

"Sorry," she said, and she took my hand once again, exposing a third finger. I watched as she raised her lancet. When it came down, I jerked back. The lancet stuck in the wooden top of the dresser, and Mrs. Mead exclaimed in a harsh tone.

There was a lot of arm wrestling after that. She got my drop of blood, but the irony of it all was that the results of the test came back negative. Still no one could explain why I kept getting sick. Even more perplexing, others had begun to get the fevers. In fact, the disease kept spreading until there seemed to be a small epidemic. Dozens of kids lay on their bunk beds, tossing and sweating. Alarmed, Mrs. Mead quit poking children in the finger and requested help. My father was brought to Addis to assess the situation.

The Friday afternoon that Dad and Mom showed up at Bingham, I wasn't at my usual sentry post in the cedar. I felt almost shocked to lift my eyes from a book and see them standing in my dorm room — as if they had sneaked up and caught me doing something I shouldn't.

Dad explained that he was here to help treat the children with fevers. Mom said she was sorry I had been sick so much. They took Johnathan and me to the mission guesthouse for the weekend, and on the way they stopped to shop for us at the Mercado downtown. I felt indifferent about everything at first, as if caring were too much work. However, when Mom bought me a bright yellow windbreaker with a sporty stripe down the front, and when she said that she would sew our country badges onto it — the ones we had collected while passing through Europe between mission terms — I told her that would be nice. I would like that.

I told them about the book I had read — the one about Andrew Jackson and the British soldier who slashed him with a sword. When we got to the guesthouse, though, I retreated into myself again. I hated how all the other adults crowded around my parents as soon as we entered the dining hall. All of them talked so easily and familiarly with my mother and father, or they doted on my little brother, Nat. They wanted to swap news about medical shipments and biblical translations. Worse yet, one of them began quizzing me about what it was like to be an eight-year-old going to boarding school.

"What have you liked best this year?" the elderly nurse asked, to which there seemed to be no polite answer. Maybe leaving? Or being asleep? Or climbing the cedar and disappearing?

"I don't know," I mumbled.

Only after dinner were we allowed to talk to Mom and Dad apart from the rest of the missionary community, and I began to feel a bit more natural. By bedtime I was goofing around a little with Nat, burrowing under the covers of one of the beds and turning it into a cave.

"Lord, please help Timmy to feel better soon and not have fevers," Mother prayed after we had settled down in our separate cots.

I shivered in the delicious cool of the sheets, pressed down by the heavy wool blankets. An organ sighed in the chapel downstairs, where the same elderly nurse from dinner was practicing a hymn. "Trust and obey," she warbled, sending her voice up through the loose wooden floorboards, "for there's no other way, to be happy in Jesus, but to trust and obey."

Mother went on, "And please take care of Grandmother Conrad. Help her to feel better."

"What's the matter with Grandma?" I asked before Mom could go further. I tried with difficulty to remember the little wispy-haired lady whom we had visited a few times when we were on furlough in Kansas City.

"She's sick in the heart," Nat boasted, pleased that he knew something his older brothers didn't know. "She even had to go to the hospital."

"Is she going to die?" I asked Mom.

"Oh, c'mon," Johnathan muttered from his bed.

Nat butted in: "Maybe she won't die. That's what Daddy said."

"I didn't ask you," I shot back.

Mom sighed. Car lights flashed from the street outside, momentarily lighting up the window and illuminating her weary white cheeks, her fingers kneading her forehead.

"She's doing better, Timmy. But we need to keep praying for her because she still doesn't feel very well and she's all alone. Now no more interruptions."

So we prayed for Grandma, whom I tried to picture in black-and-white photographic images, downy white hair in a halo around her head. We also prayed for Sisoni Odeiki, our orphan in Indonesia, whom we had been supporting for four years with small donations sent to World Vision.

A gregarious bachelor-missionary had delayed Dad when he took his toothbrush down the hall to the communal bathroom. After Dad tiptoed back into the room, he leaned over each of us to kiss us on the cheek, his whiskers scratchy, his breath minty. "I love you," he whispered in my ear, "and God loves you too." He stayed by my bed, leaning over and rubbing my head, scratching at the scalp. For a long time, he stayed there, and after he stepped away, I lay awake, relishing the cheerful honking of taxis on Churchill Boulevard and the car lights sweeping the ceiling. I savored the sensation of my family lying all around me in the dark, so close that I could hear their breathing and feel the warmth of it in the air.

The next morning, Mom took me down to the playground behind the main building, where the passion fruit vines wove their way along the stone wall and long-stemmed orange flowers burst out of dark green fronds. It was there that the accident happened. I hollered at her to watch me leap off a rock pile into a cedar tree. I wanted to show her how well I could climb, how high I could go. But another missionary lady walked up at the same moment and asked her a question.

Mother nodded at me absentmindedly and turned away. "She's doing better now, thank you. She's almost out of the hospital."

I still jumped, but I was so fixed on getting Mom's attention that I forgot to watch the branch I was jumping to. My wrists whacked the limb. My hands didn't catch. When my feet flew up in the air, I dropped back headfirst — right onto the rock pile.

The next thing I knew I was leaning forward in a bathtub, still clothed, with Mom supporting me under the armpits. Warm water was dripping off the back of my head where Dad had shaved a patch of my scalp so that he could sew me up. I could feel the tug of a needle, strangely painless due to local anesthetic. Then Dad sat me up and gave me a hand mirror and turned me around with my back to the bathroom mirror so I could see all the little threads poking out like hog bristles.

"You'll have a scar to boast about," he said. "That's for sure."

It took Dad another day or two of medical sleuthing to come up with a theory for the fevers that had hit Bingham. After consulting with Mrs. Mead and looking at her blood tests, and after doing some of his own blood work and quizzing children, he finally announced what he thought was causing the disease: our pet pigeons.

He believed the epidemic had started when one of the older

boys was spitting grain into the beak of an infected bird. Then it had spread from child to child. Maybe I had even gotten the fever from my hours in the cedar tree, nibbling on contaminated grain. What this meant, Dad announced, was that all the Bingham pigeons would have to go!

There was a general outcry. Dozens of boys kept pigeons, even my brother Jonathan, and all of them were terribly attached to their pets. Johnathan's pigeon, aptly named Charlie Brown, was slow-witted, but he and I both loved it, in part because it needed so much caretaking. I liked to watch my brother toss the bird gently into the air — how it would flutter clumsily, regaining the use of its wings. After circling once or twice, Charlie almost always came back to perch, unless he was feeling particularly brave, in which case he would wing his way over the school fence, disappearing for a few minutes before making a dramatic return. It was fun to imagine where he had gone. To give him up seemed like such a shame now, since he had survived a series of misfortunes: reappearing after two days AWOL, then getting so wet in a storm that he crash-landed in the garbage pit behind the gym and had to be rescued by a boy on a rope. Nonetheless, despite Charlie's miraculous escapes, now he and his feathered comrades were doomed.

The birds were packed into a large wire box by the Ethiopian groundskeeper. Then they were driven up the mountain road beyond Addis, taken by one of the single teachers and the groundskeeper. There, they were shooed into the forest, clapping their wings in panic and wobbling around on the ground. To keep them from coming back, the cage at the gym had to be torn down, and all the feed grain had to be thrown in the garbage pit. Everyone was warned not to touch or feed pigeons.

My brother, like all the other kids at Bingham, could hardly bear this loss, but it was doubly appalling for him and me because now we had to hear our classmates' criticisms about Dad, which felt like a judgment on us. After a week, when Mom and Dad and Nat had left for home, the grumbling died down. Life at school returned to normal for the most part. However, the old routine didn't feel so familiar or secure anymore. I could no longer go a full day without thinking of my parents or Nat or our home at Leimo.

One evening, a boy teased me, making fun of how bald I was back where the stitches still poked out of my shaved head.

"Baldy, baldy, baldy," he chanted.

I had never really liked this boy, Norris, who had a spray of pitch-black hair, a lean face, and a tendency to point out weaknesses. But right now I didn't like anything. Not the dorm room we were in. Not the kids standing around waiting to see if I would react. Not the pukey green paint or the thought of porridge for breakfast.

He was still standing there sneering, so I threw a punch. When he swung back, I dove into him and butted him to the ground. We rolled, each of us trying to get on top. My head banged against the linoleum, but I hardly noticed. Soon I was on top and thrashing at him. Then I saw blood, a big smear of it on the floor. I kept swinging, trying to figure out where the blood had come from. His nose wasn't bleeding, nor was mine. I didn't stop until I heard Mrs. Johnson shouting and felt her pulling at my collar. Her face was blanched. Norris's was flushed, but he kept glancing, wide-eyed, at something just behind my ear. I put my hand up there and it came back scarlet.

It took another week for the wound to seal. Then Mrs. Mead pulled the stitches. My hair grew back in. Mom and Dad wrote, happy to hear that I was getting better and happy to hear that the other kids who had been sick were out of bed. For a few weeks, it seemed that the whole epidemic was a bad memory. The classrooms were full. Everyone seemed healthy—all of them, that is, but me.

Once again, I became sick, so sick that I had to walk slowly to the toilet, keeping one hand on the wall just to be sure I didn't tip. I fell so far behind in my schoolwork that Miss Willey wasn't sure she could help me catch up. She did something that had never occurred to me as an option: with a few weeks left in the term, she recommended that I be sent home.

• • •

So it was that I spent the remainder of third grade at home with my parents and Nat, living in the little stucco house at Leimo. At Christmas, Johnathan came home too, but I was still suffering from the fevers, so he was sent back to Bingham alone after the holidays. I began to study under my mother's care, completing my exercises in half the time due to her one-on-one tutoring.

Some days I still got sick, spiking a fever. In fact, once Dad had to put me on intravenous fluids, as I was close to dehydration. During that time, I dreamed that I was being shipped back to the academy in a careening bus. Chickens and goats stepped into the path of the hurtling vehicle only to be struck aside. The driver was determined to continue at the same absurd speed, even though passengers screamed for him to stop: "*A-kum! A-kum!*"

When I woke in distress and forgot the intravenous needle, I nearly pulled it out of my arm while lurching toward the coffee can that served as my bedpan. I felt disoriented and tormented, standing in the dark in my sweaty PJs with a stabbing pain in the crook of my arm.

Yet . . . just as unexpectedly as each fever struck, it also faded. I would begin to feel better and get up. On "well" days, as soon as I had finished schoolwork, I could pretty much do as I pleased. I would put on the yellow windbreaker that Mom had bought me in Addis, fingering the country badges she had sewn across the chest, as promised. Then I would take Nat to gather tadpoles in the grassy puddles behind the hospital. Or I would bring him with me and wander through the patient ward, watching Dad as he cared for the strange people in their beds, their legs in casts, their chests sunken with tuberculosis, their faces tight on their skulls.

Sometimes, if Nat was sleeping or playing with the Dyes's youngest children, I would go away all on my own and climb the huge eucalyptus on the edge of our compound, going as high as I could, where I liked to sit in the windy sky, unnoticed but able to see home not far away.

"Look, Mom," I yelled as she came to the garden to get lettuce or strawberries. "I'm over here."

She waved back. "Tim, how did you get so high? You be careful!"

Although I stayed alone up there, staring out over the Leimo station and the river valley below, I felt different than I had felt in the cedar at Bingham. I felt solid and alive. I especially felt that way every time Mom saw me in the tree and called out.

"I know," I shouted back to her. "Don't worry. I'm holding on."

Warning Signs

IN THE MORNING AT LEIMO, I liked to lie in bed just enjoying the fact that I was there. Usually the Dyes operated the radio, since Mr. Dye was the station head, but Mom handled it a few times while they were away. On those days I listened from my bed as she reported to headquarters, ending each sentence with the word *over* and sometimes spelling out names or prescriptions or other difficult words with code words: *Alpha* for *A*, *Bravo* for *B*, and so on.

Mom closed with our assigned call letters: "This is 9 Echo, Echo, 52, signing off. Over and out." Then she clicked off the radio to save power in the car battery that fueled it — unless she wanted to listen to just one more station, catching the crackly voice of another missionary at Soddo or Jimma or Shashamane, or even Bulki, high in the mountains near Kenya.

The other missionaries had interesting requests to make: "We need a fan belt to be brought on the next Cessna." "Could a telegram be sent to New York about our arrival date on Pan Am?" "Could someone buy and deliver three pairs of size twelve underwear to our son at Bingham?"

Headquarters tended to field requests rather than making comments, but occasionally something important needed to be communicated back as well. "Prayer alert. More disturbances at the Addis University. Nothing major, but pray for stability. Over."

So I found out that the students were at it again. That would mean more riot drills at Bingham, I supposed. I wondered how my brother was doing, and Danny too.

We drove up to Addis at midterm, just to check on Johnathan, but when Dad went over from headquarters to get him, I chose to stay with Mom and Nat. I didn't want to go through those gates and risk not getting back out.

After Dad returned with Johnathan, we all went to meet with a visiting friend of my parents: a woman named Joyce, who was touring Africa as part of her work. She had been close to Mom and Dad back when they first started thinking about the mission field, and now she was an ordained Presbyterian minister working for the World Council of Churches in Geneva.

We ate lasagna at the Wabashebele hotel. I felt guilty with the fine linen napkin in my lap. Academy children didn't get to eat at the Wabashebele unless they learned all their verses, and I had not had to learn verses all this term — unlike Johnathan, who had been doing it every day.

I glanced over at my older brother. Since he was eating quietly, I ate quietly. I just listened as Mom and Dad fielded Joyce's questions. She wanted to know how landlords treated tenants in the Leimo area, and how much land was owned by those who did the actual farming. "What would you guess are the percentages?" she asked.

But Mom and Dad didn't have an answer. They confirmed that there were landlords, but they could only guess at the number of farmers who owned the land they worked.

"Well, I'm curious because I've been looking at reports on human rights, and Ethiopia doesn't have a good track record," Joyce continued. "I mean, it's amazing how much of the country is actually owned by the Emperor or someone in the ruling tribe."

Mom and Dad resisted politely, pointing out that the Emperor had always been quite fair with the mission and that some of these reports might be skewed because lately university students were protesting everything imaginable. They had just rioted at a fashion show, of all things, claiming that it was cultural imperialism. They were starting to talk like Marxists.

"They probably *are* Marxists!" Joyce said.

"But why?" Mom asked. "It's a borrowed system. It's not Ethiopian at all."

"If Marxism helps to explain what they are experiencing, then of course they'll turn to it. People have been doing it all over the world. Look at Vietnam."

Dad shook his head and tried to explain the mission's policy: "Basically, we stay out of politics. If we can stay neutral, then we won't be seen as taking sides."

Joyce shot back at him. "C'mon, Charlie. Neutral? How can anyone be neutral? If the mission doesn't have a stance, then it's supporting the government. That's the real message."

I was surprised, and I could tell they were surprised too. Missionaries usually didn't talk so bluntly. In Mom's case, she sighed as if it was all too painful to discuss. But Dad seemed energized.

"It may look that way," he said, "but staying neutral at least keeps us in the country, able to do our work. I mean, we're not here for politics. We came for spiritual reasons. Give unto Caesar what is Caesar's."

Joyce smirked, as if she knew that he knew that this couldn't be the whole picture.

Dad smiled, suggesting that she might be a bit too sure of herself. Then he took an unexpected tangent. "That reminds me, Kay, I don't think I even got a chance to tell you what Erago said before we came up here."

Mom shook her head, so he went on, explaining for Joyce's benefit: "Erago is the chaplain at our hospital, and his brother is a nurse at the Russian hospital in Addis. Anyway, he told me on the way to the plane that I should keep my eyes open in Addis because, according to his brother, the Russians are up to something."

He was grinning and Mom could tell he was treating this news as a joke. She raised an eyebrow and reprimanded him, "Charles, this is serious."

He opened both eyes wide, protesting his innocence. "What? I'm just telling you what Erago said. They've got a plan. It's all being masterminded from here. From the Russian hospital in Addis."

At that point, Joyce shook a finger at Dad. Then she leaned across toward Mom and patted her on the shoulder. "I'll be praying for you, Kay."

"Please do," Mom replied.

That's when Nat asked what exactly the Russians were planning, which put a cap on the whole topic. I was disappointed. After all, it wasn't every day that I got to listen as adults discussed secret plots and possible spies. But now that they saw how closely we had been listening, they put the politics away and went back to eating their lasagna.

A conversation like that one — with someone outside the mission circle — brought out a dimension of my parents' personalities that didn't often come to the surface. Rarely did I see them acting so unguarded when we were at Leimo, where everyone had to work together "cheek-to-jowl," as Mom put it. When we returned to the mission station, Mom and Dad hunkered down and kept their thoughts to themselves.

During my slow recuperation, I had never fully recovered my usual level of energy. On the best days, I could take only small forays out-of-doors, bringing Nat with me. We climbed into the tree house, or we pulled up grass to cover over the drainage ditch below the garden, which allowed us to crawl around, imagining drama without expending the energy necessary for running. We liked to pretend we were spies. We put on matching green sweatshirts and pulled up the hoods, so that we would be invisible in our hiding places. We particularly liked to spy on our new gardener, who had been hired after the old gardener said he needed to spend more time on his farm.

This new gardener was younger and less friendly. A lean man with wide canvas shorts and a faded *shamma,* he always arrived at the house clutching a spear. He said very little, except to answer Mom's instructions with a quiet yes — *"ishie."* For the first few weeks, he ignored Nat and me. Then, one afternoon when he saw us watching, he called us over and offered me his hoe, pointing at the ground with his chin. When I tried to use the tool, he laughed.

I was useless. I couldn't even break the ground. He would have to show me the way it was done. He put his hands over mine, bringing the hoe down in a chopping motion so that the turf tore and fell away in chunks. He kept my hands under his own for twenty or thirty chops, even though my fingers hurt and my arms jerked out of control. Then he took the hoe back and went down the row with his back to us, hacking the ground in a steady rhythm, breaking it into smaller and smaller clods.

We liked to spy on the new gardener because he seemed slightly dangerous and because he seemed to enjoy our attention. We sneaked across the backyard, hugging the side of the storage shed, then quickly crawled into the drainage ditch near the garden. When we peeked out, lifting the grass ceiling of our hiding place, he was carrying a bucket of water from the barrel under our downspout or cropping lettuce with a knife. He acted completely absorbed in his tasks, until just the moment when we relaxed our guard and quit watching. Then *thunk* — a clod hit the ground near us. We looked back, but no matter how quick we were, we always found him concentrating on his work again, pulling weeds out of the corn or shoveling manure onto the new area he had hoed.

The only time that the new gardener actually came looking for us was when he was about to butcher a chicken. Then, oddly, he sought us out, finding us in the Dyes's yard or behind the hospital, and telling us in Amharic to follow him: *"Lidgeoch, inaheed."*

He put grain in our hands and pushed us toward the selected hen. Then he stalked it from behind. As the bird approached, pecking at the grain we had spilled, he swooped in and snatched it into the air, hanging it upside down by its scaly yellow legs. The hen flapped and flapped, trying to right itself. Only after it had quieted did he reach out with his free hand and caress its beak. Then he kept on stroking that beak as he walked it to the back of our storage shed and eased it down slowly over the stump that served as a chopping block.

The hen's head rested sideways on the wood, blinking lazily, hypnotized by the moving finger; and at this point the gardener grinned wickedly. He invited us to come touch the bird. Once, I did, but usually I hung back, shaking my head, which made him smile more. I was mesmerized, as was Nat. We watched with horrid fascination as his right hand crept away from the hen, searching for the handle of the ax, and as he raised the sharp wedge and brought it down with a clap.

This was the moment Nat and I had been waiting for. No matter how many times the gardener acted out this ritual, we could never be prepared for what happened, which was why we always came back to watch, willing but apprehensive. We were drawn back by our own morbid desire for a kind of pulsing, shrieking excitement.

The headless hen became a panicked burst of feathers, with blood spurting. The gardener tossed it away like a sack. It bounced on the ground, took steps, fell over, lifted into the air again on crazed wings. It flew straight at us, breast matted with blood, and we ran screaming as it veered away then thunked into the wall of the storage shed. When we looked back, it was hanging upside down in a bush, flapping in slow motion, still acting out its last thought. Then it twitched and hung dead.

The head on the chopping block had not moved. It peered at us with an open eye. The gardener picked it up and motioned as if he would toss it our way. We screamed again and ran, and he laughed. This childish fear was a source of great satisfaction to him. He loved to raise it up in us. But when Mom came out later, to check on the plucking and the gutting, he was always so sober, so quiet, so very respectful.

During those months of my convalescence, when my only real contact with the local community was through our gardener, a problem began to emerge in the larger relationship between the mission and the people of Leimo. Cattle herders kept herding cattle across the compound, leaving wet dung in front of the hospital and presenting potential hazards to children if a bullock got loose. Dad and Mr. Dye became concerned enough that they discussed marking off the whole compound with a fence. After all, dung carried disease, and what if Nat or little Cathy got trampled?

They finally took action, going to work alongside our gardener, digging fence holes in a long line and setting the posts in place, ready to be tamped down. In a single day, they had it ready to erect. They stood back, pleased with their work. Tomorrow, they would string the wire.

However, in the morning, when Dad stepped out of the house, he groaned and put his head back in the door. "Kathryn, come take a look!"

Nat and I came running too, curious to see what could cause such a reaction. We all stood on the porch stunned. Every post had been tossed aside, and all the dirt had been put back in the holes.

"Who do you think did it?" I asked.

Dad stared at the scattered posts, shaking his head wearily. "It could be anyone. Absolutely anyone."

"Maybe you should dig the holes again and let Nat and me spy on them. We could watch from the tree house."

He patted me on the back. "And then what would you do?"

"We'd tell you."

A boy of twelve or thirteen had just crossed the unfinished fence line, walking behind a pair of loose-skinned oxen. He whacked them on the hips as they tried to stop and graze. The oxen lifted their heads and moved on, ambling past our porch. Then the boy looked up and called out very boldly, like an adult, "*Ttuma.*"

Dad lifted his head in acknowledgment but simply watched as the boy whacked the oxen across the compound. When he spoke, it was as if he was talking to no one in particular. He smiled wryly. "Well, one thing you have to say for people here. They aren't pushovers."

Lost Armor

THIRD GRADE ENDED with me still at home being taught by Mom. When only a month remained, I began to look forward to Johnathan's return from Bingham Academy, even though that reminded me that I would have to go back to boarding school after the holidays.

"Charles," Mom said one night, while putting Nat and me into bed, "don't you think it's time to tell the boys?"

Dad didn't seem to register her words, gazing down between his feet at the dark floor of our bedroom.

"Charles?"

"Kathryn!" he shot back.

He peered across the candlelit room at her flickering face, which seemed caught in exaggerated shock, eyebrows lifted, everything lit up from below. Then he swung his head toward Nat and me. "Your mother and I have been talking about whether we should go back to the States for a bit."

This news came as a complete surprise. I propped myself up on an elbow: "But why? I thought we had to stay for three years, not two."

Dad didn't answer, so Mom gave her explanation: "We've just decided we need a break, that's all. And the mission agreed."

"How come?"

"Lots of reasons. Your Grandma is still sick, so we'd like to see her. You have been sick a lot too. And your Dad has been working very hard . . ."

She glanced across the room toward Dad, who had tipped back in his chair and was staring out the window, face raised toward the full moon. His sturdy, chiseled features seemed to sag a bit in the silver light, broken by dents of darkness around the eyes and in the hollows of his cheeks.

"Will I go to a different school?" I asked.

"Probably not," Mom offered. "We're hoping to stay only a few months."

"Can we go on a plane?" Nat asked.

"C'mon," I hissed. "How else are we going to get there?"

"That is *not* the way to talk to your brother," Mom interjected. "Besides, missionaries used to take ships."

"Maybe a long time ago."

I risked pushing right to the edge of this argument because I secretly wanted Dad to get involved, but he remained removed, speaking only briefly. He forgot to say good night, so Mom had to lead prayers and do all the tucking in. A bit later, after they had gone to the living room, I could hear Mom trying to coax him into conversation, using a deliberately cheerful voice. His mumbled responses stuck in the walls of the house, but snippets of her pep talk came through.

"She's only one perspective, Charles, and she's probably threatened. Since you're the doctor, she may . . ."

He mumbled and she broke back in, "I know, but she's like that; she's always saying what's on her mind . . ."

Marie again. It still baffled me how this one woman could have such power over my father — and how she could seem so nice at times. This was the woman who had let Nat and me come to her bungalow to play Chinese checkers during the past few weeks. And yet she was also the one who wouldn't look at Dad when he talked to her. Marie invited us to tasting parties when she cranked ice cream; yet she had told my father he didn't belong in Ethiopia. How could both people exist in the same body?

"She's ignoring the evidence," Mom insisted on the other side of the bedroom wall. "You've accomplished a great deal. That hospital was a locked-up wreck. Don't you remember? We had to sweep bird droppings out of the operating room . . ."

Some more mumbling and a pause. "But, Charles, you've helped thousands. You've done what a lot of doctors could never do. Don't let one person change that."

His voice tailed off again, and Mom interjected, "You don't know that. Besides, if we take a furlough, maybe she'll get reassigned . . ."

Dad laughed in a forced, bitter voice.

"OK, then maybe *we'll* get reassigned. Even that would be better, wouldn't it?"

Three weeks later, having packed our dishes and books into wooden crates in the storage shed — the same one that the Esterline family had used as a temporary house during the Hosanna school revolt — we left Leimo, carrying four suitcases. This time, there was little of the hoopla that had accompanied our departure from Soddo: no gifts from the house helpers and no special gatherings of the mission staff.

The adults hugged, looking awkward. Nat and I shook hands with the kids. Then I patted our horse, Gillian, on the shoulder and told him goodbye. He just kept on grazing. He didn't lift his head. And as we got into the Land Rover with Mr. Dye to be driven to the airstrip at Hosanna, everyone acted very normal, as if we were leaving on a supply run to Addis and would be back in a week. Mom didn't even cry.

A few days later, after picking up Jonathan in Addis and making jet-lagged stops in Rome and Amsterdam, we found ourselves back on American soil, standing in the John F. Kennedy Airport. While Mom and Dad debriefed with the heads of the mission, we stayed in New York City, rooming at the national headquarters for the Sudan Interior Mission — an old tenement building that had been saved from the wrecking ball. We had stayed there the last time we returned on furlough, and when my parents had tried to take us on a walk, I had actually clung to a street sign. At the age of six, I'd hardly seen a stoplight in action, so I didn't trust that a single red light could halt a cascade of New York taxis. Now, though, I was a nine-year-old veteran — a boarding-school survivor and world traveler. I had not only seen stoplights, I had seen them in strange cities on the other side of the globe too. In fact, my bright yellow windbreaker had cloth badges sewn onto it from a half-dozen countries, including a new badge from Rome with a red-and-black coat of arms, as well as badges from Athens and Zurich and Amsterdam. How many nine-year-olds could boast a jacket like that?

Remarkably, two of Mom and Dad's closest college friends, also missionaries, were in New York City at the same time, about to return to the Congo. A year earlier, a guerrilla rebellion had forced the Youmans to flee with their children from a station in the central rain forest of the Congo. Now they were returning because Roger had been asked to take charge of the medical staff at the huge Kinshasa General Hospital.

We joined them for a trip to the Statue of Liberty. Their daughters, Joy and Grace, with lustrous blond ponytails, gave the outing an extra electric energy. Johnathan and I raced the girls to the top, and as I pounded up the iron stairs, I enjoyed the bouncing of my voice and the booming echo of my feet. I reached the observation deck just behind Johnathan. I poked my head out of a square window in the lady's crown. Then I shouted as loud as the others, declaring my independence to the pigeons that circled the great spiked head, to the ferryboat waiting for us down below, and to the distant skyscrapers needling the sky. I wasn't afraid of New York City or the huge continent in front of me. I wasn't afraid of anything now. I was the boy who had survived Africa.

I kept that tough-guy attitude all the way back on the ferryboat and across Manhattan Island to the mission headquarters. But when we sat down to supper in the cafeteria, I realized I had left my windbreaker on the ferry, and something collapsed inside of me. With the loss of that jacket and all its traveling badges went some deeper sense of meaning, of identity. Who was I anyway, this half-African, half-American creature, this missionary Gypsy brought to America? I cried until I couldn't cry anymore, and when I fell asleep, I slept like the dead, not waking until midday. I felt very small in the noonday light, lying in a foreign bed in a foreign city, overwhelmed by the cataract of engine noises at my window.

Here we were now, ten stories up in New York City, where pigeons kept startling us at the windows and other people could be seen looking across at us from their own rooms like zoo animals on display. For a minute I just lay there, overwhelmed by my own sense of loss. Mom was flipping through old photos, preparing a scrapbook to show family and friends and people at supporting churches, so I watched her with half-interest.

"Ouch," she said after a minute, shaking her head over one black-and-white shot in a sad but amused way.

I asked to see the photo, and she brought it over to me. Although it had been taken in Greece while we were on our way to Ethiopia, it seemed to represent everything about our last term as a missionary family. While touring an amphitheater in Greece, we had flopped down on hot stone benches, and a roving photographer had caught us as we truly were — physically together but locked in separate miseries. Five-year-old Nat, who hated bright sunlight and cameras, was scowling at the photographer, face contorted. Johnathan, curled up between Mom and Dad with his elbow on Dad's thigh, peered intently at a set of photographic slides, as if these other images were more compelling than the reality around him. And me? Seated on Dad's other leg, with one eye squeezed shut, I stared out of the frame, completely unimpressed with the ancient dust, the waiting, the incomprehensible nature of our journey.

The only ones who seemed somewhat connected in this photo were Mom and Dad. Mom, with her hair tousled by the wind, was looking over at Dad with her hand crooked under her chin, as if fingering an invisible necklace. Dad, who was supporting both Johnathan and me in his lap, had his elbow up on the stone backrest and his head turned back toward her. Their eyes were locked. The

THE AMPHITHEATER IN GREECE.
Separate woes.

way they looked at each other, the frankness of their gaze, suggested a kind of raw honesty that had been born out of shared difficulty, out of hard times. There was no illusion — just a stubborn sense of shared purpose, a yoked determination.

"Now that's a keeper," Dad said, looking over our shoulders, which caused Mom to bring the photo down to lunch so that she could show it to the Youmans as well. When she brought it out again in the cafeteria, Roger and Winkie broke into rollicking, sustained laughter. Mom and Dad laughed too. They all laughed until they cried. Then Mom said, "That's the way it is, isn't it? You either laugh or you cry."

I suspect my mother wanted to cry, but she kept laughing. Whenever the others started to collect themselves, she laughed again. She laughed and laughed, and as she laughed, tears dribbled down her cheeks. It was a rare laughter, an unprotected outflow of something that had been held back too long. Her complete lack of propriety was infectious. We all joined in—not just Dad and Roger and Winkie, but Johnathan and Nat and the Youmans' kids and myself. We sighed and hooted and slapped at each other and wiped our eyes. And it was both wonderfully freeing and, after a while, frightening.

The brief moment of silence that followed felt full of unvoiced thoughts, full of a shared, telepathic meaning that only our two families could understand.

We would not return to Ethiopia this time. We were technically on medical leave, scheduled to finish our three-year term as soon as we had spent sufficient time with Mom's ailing mother. However, after we arrived in Hiawatha, Kansas, and rented an attic apartment across the street from Grandmother Clara, my parents admitted to themselves that this was not just a medical leave.

In December 1969, after a half-year of treading water, my father took a job in a nearby Kansas town fifteen miles from Saint Joseph, Missouri, the city where I had been born. Dad agreed to become the doctor for this town, Troy, and for the outlying farm communities that lay in that northeast corner of Kansas, nestled in a curve of the Missouri River.

The move to Troy seemed like just another change at first, and I was tired of changes. I remember becoming so angry at my brothers and the closeness of our space that one day I ran right through our screen door, tearing a hole in it. On another occasion, when Nat changed the channels on the TV, I smacked him across the back with a plastic sword, raising a welt.

I couldn't sleep, either. At night, especially if Mom and Dad were away at one of the neighborhood Bible study groups they were helping to start, I lay in my bed waiting to hear our Plymouth in the driveway. Not until I could hear that engine reverberating up through the frame of the house, and not until I could feel the soft *whump* of the front door being shut behind my tiptoeing parents, would I let go and sleep.

Worried by my sleeplessness and by my complaint of constant

headaches, Mom and Dad took me to Kansas City to see a neurologist, who glued electrodes to my scalp as I lay on a gurney. He told me to go to sleep, which I found very hard to do given the circumstances. When I woke, he had me look at a lot of inkblots, and I found that more enjoyable. There was no clear diagnosis, though. No treatment either. I still got the headaches. I still slammed doors and broke rakes and lay for thirty minutes at a time underneath my bed, down with the rusted springs and the drifts of lint.

Then, after a bit, I began to control my outbursts. Gradually, I began to anger less quickly. And I slept better. The fact that we settled down in Troy — not just a year or two, but longer — and the fact that I kept coming home every day from school, finding my parents and my brothers still there, began to have a calming, reassuring effect.

News from Ethiopia was rare in our little town, but occasionally one of my parents' acquaintances dropped by on furlough and brought us a report. They said the riots had worsened. A group of new young leaders had gained enough support to set up a separate government, functioning alongside the ancient monarchy. These leaders — who called themselves a "Committee of Equals," or *Derg* — had promised to remain loyal to the Emperor. However, our friends told us that key members of parliament had been arrested. We heard that the central court had been dissolved, then that the airport was shut down. No one could go anywhere in Addis because all the taxi drivers refused to drive.

The unthinkable finally happened on September 12, 1974. Three soldiers came to the Emperor's palace and took away Haile Selassie, the Lion of Judah, putting him in the back seat of a Volkswagen Bug. Ethiopia was declared a Marxist state.

After that climactic day, Mom and Dad would sometimes give us other updates, letting us know that a large group of parliamentary leaders had been executed, or that one of the *Derg* members named Colonel Mengistu had taken command of the *Derg* by imprisoning or executing most of the other committee members. They told me, a year later, that Emperor Selassie had died, either due to cardiac arrest or suffocation with a pillow, depending on whom one believed.

When I heard about his death, I was reminded of my childhood dream in Soddo: the Emperor on the cliff, looking down, pointing out over an abyss I refused to approach. I remembered the wind whipping his cape, and I remembered how afraid I was that he might be blown over the edge, or that I might tumble after him. But those social upheavals, so distant now, and so abstract, couldn't displace my own sense of Ethiopia — the land that I had gained and lost several times over, the home that could never fully be home. And I did not dwell on the news because now I was busy becoming an American boy — a Kansas boy in a small town where almost every family had relatives from the previous two or three generations. I had to work hard at being here, but maybe I had a chance this time. If we stayed long enough, maybe I could finally belong.

Epilogue

AFTER SIX YEARS in Troy, Kansas, our family did return again to Ethiopia. We arrived in 1977, at the height of the Marxist revolution—a period later called "The Red Terror." This was not the Ethiopia we had known. The mission church, suspected for its association with "imperialistic" nations like the United States, was under persecution. Church members were being dragged off to prison and torture. Many churches were boarded shut, even burned.

We had to face our own fears as soldiers bullied us at check points or seized mission properties, taking away the hospital at Soddo, forcing my parents to evacuate their mountain station in Gammu Gofa Province, far south of Leimo, and eventually commandeering the Lutheran high school I was attending so that they could turn it into a military hospital.

My father's medical work became severely restricted. He could not leave the capital unless he petitioned for a travel permit. In Addis, large paintings, three or four stories high, took over the sides of buildings, picturing the victorious Ethiopian army marching over a fallen Uncle Sam. They said in bold English: "Go Home, Yankee."

Finally, after eight months of increasing pressure, we left Ethiopia like refugees, to start over in Sudan. Once again, I had lost the country that I had tried to make my own. When I finished high school at a boarding school in Kenya, we traveled back to the United States, and I felt I had to put away my African past altogether. It was too different and strange next to the memories of my college friends. If I tried to describe the way we had lived, they had no point of reference. "Interesting" was all they could say. So I buried Ethiopia in the deep storage of my memory, deep enough that it seemed forgotten.

I didn't open up much about my childhood after that. It didn't help that I was slowly drifting away from my religious tradition. Not satisfied with the duty-oriented Christianity that I had always known and the cerebral conformity that it seemed to require, I found myself drawn toward churches that had an open, sacramental sense of God—churches where mystery was welcome, where the senses were trusted, where honest exploration was encouraged rather than feared. During that time, I fell in love with a woman who was studying to become an Episcopal priest. She had a strong sense of God appearing to her in dreams or feeding her at Communion. I realized that I wanted to experience God that way, not just clinging to religious concepts but encountering God head-on.

We married. Aside from Cathy, not many people knew about my childhood in Ethiopia. However, as sometimes happens, I was offered an unexpected opportunity to come full circle back to my childhood haunts as an adult. I took a job that involved training writers and editors with church organizations in Africa, and after visiting a half-dozen countries, I received a request to lead a workshop in Addis Ababa.

When I first flew back to Ethiopia, in 1990, the *Derg* still ruled the country and Christian churches were operating underground. My main contact, who knew my parents well, was a winsome man who could laugh at the fact that he first fell in love with his wife while they were prisoners, shaved bald, in a mass prison for religious dissidents.

I returned to Ethiopia a second time in 1991 to offer more training. Two weeks before my arrival, Tigrean and Eritrean rebels from the north had fought their way into Addis, ousting the *Derg* and promising a democratic government. This time, when our family friend, Ato Sahle, drove me to his house, we had to skirt a scorched tank with a turret that hung askew. His children told me about lying on the floor and singing Psalm 23 — *Yea though I walk through the valley of the shadow of death, I shall fear no evil* — as artillery shells whistled overhead.

I came back one last time in 1994, soon after my wife and I had witnessed the birth of our first son. Paradoxically, my parents were also back in the country for a short-term mission, and the workshop I was leading had been organized by our mutual friend, Sahle Tilahun, now head of a Baptist publishing house and respected widely for having stayed true to his faith during the Marxist persecution.

The site Sahle had chosen for our editorial workshop was the one place I most wanted to return to — the retreat center at Lake Bishoftu. For a full week, I stayed in one of the cabins on the slope, walking down to the screened hut by the lake. Between workshop sessions, I paddled out onto the water, reliving the happy things that I had done as a child with my family: scooting into the reedy tunnels to look for weaverbird nests, chasing snakebirds, stopping out there in the middle of the wide expanse to rock on the waves, eyes closed, as I listened to the slap and gurgle under the boat.

The Marxists had forbidden Christian editors and writers to publish Christian material, since atheism was state policy. Now a number of underground Christian publications were coming above ground, and the editors wanted to expand their reach. For them, writing was a tool, useful mainly for evangelism. It had a utilitarian value — like the milled lumber that made a house. For me, on the other hand, writing was like the living tree that had preceded the planks or the building. I did not like to see it forced into predetermined agendas or notions of Truth.

Even more difficult for me was the way that some of the Christian writers and editors used writing as a weapon. For them, the pen was truly mightier than a sword, so they wielded it like a sword — to persuade, to defend, to attack, always to win. Their approach to publishing brought back the militaristic beat of my childhood — "Onward, Christian soldiers, marching as to war." And it brought back a quiet distrust of what seemed, to me, like a kind of spiritual imperialism.

However, given what these editors and writers had been through, each of them personally impacted by the persecution of the Marxist *Derg*, I could understand why writing might feel like war and why they were ready to engage in the battle. They saw the potential for literature to be life-changing, and they were willing to risk their lives on that premise, so I did what I could to help them defend what seemed worthwhile.

On the last evening of the workshop, we roasted a goat down by the lake, where the tethered rowboats and canoes knocked against the wooden dock. Little waves lapped into the boathouse where my brother Johnathan and I had eased into Lake Bishoftu for the first time. The roasted goat was a seasoned delight. Stars glittered. Everyone had stories to tell, and no person more than Ato Sahle.

No longer was Sahle the timid teen my parents had met at the gate of Debre Birhan Language School. He now had flecks of silver in his hair and a playful smile that suggested all of life might be amusing in the end. He spoke very fondly of my parents. He told the other editors how he had traveled with my father during the worst part of the Marxist era. After several stops, the fan belt had broken on the Land Rover, so Sahle and Dad and the two nurses had to create makeshift substitutes out of shoestrings and belts and finally a nurse's pantyhose. When the first gear broke as well, they pushed the car into second gear and leapt in.

That night, when they stopped at a Seventh-day Adventist mission far from any major town or city, Dad and Sahle slept in the same borrowed hut, side by side. "Uncle Charlie was very tired," Sahle said. "We just lay there and talked in the darkness. It was very nice, I tell you. Almost like sleeping. And then he asked me, 'Well ... why don't we pray?' I was very much surprised, you know, because it was not my custom to pray lying down. It seemed disrespectful, maybe. 'Do you think it is OK?' I asked. But your daddy, he says he thinks that God will hear us no matter whether we are standing or lying."

Ato Sahle laughed softly, his face alive with the memory. "I tell you, it was very nice. We prayed a long time, just talking as if we were talking with a friend. To tell you the truth, Tim, your father — your mother too — they were good missionaries. I have known many missionaries, but never anyone like them. Still they are like family to me."

I listened to Ato Sahle with a strange mixture of pride and pain. I had been at boarding school when he took that epic journey with my father. Once again I had been out of my parents' picture while other people — Sahle included — were *in* the picture. My parents' desire to reach out — to embrace everyone — this was the thing that had taken them out of my own reach. It was also the thing that had removed me from the Ethiopian culture, cordoned off in a fenced school in Addis Ababa.

Nevertheless, I appreciated hearing this high compliment from Sahle, not just because of how it confirmed my parents' openness to the people of Ethiopia, but how it confirmed my own new connection to the same people. I was finally part of the circle, included. So often as a child I had been cut off from Ethiopians by circumstance or by resentful reaction. In fact, when I looked back, I had to admit, embarrassed, that I could not name a single Ethiopian playmate. But now, as I sat in the dark with this group of good men and women at the goat roast by Lake Bishoftu, I felt connected to them in a new and real way. I felt surprisingly connected to my parents as well.

The next morning, at the end of the workshop, I was presented with a full traditional costume — white jodhpurs and white tunic and white wraparound *shamma*. I looked anemic swaddled in all that white, but I received a battery of compliments as Sahle took pictures of me standing next to the Botswanian editor who had helped to lead the training. Isaac looked very handsome, standing

ISAAC AND ME AT LAKE BISHOFTU.
My new clothes.

in his identical outfit. He was black and white in high contrast. I was a pale replica. But I did not feel like a pretender. I was no chameleon. I wore the outfit proudly, for I felt that I had been welcomed at last to claim my place in this land that I had lost so long ago.

"Say *'tanayistilling,'*" someone shouted, as Sahle prepared to take the photo, and I responded softly, from deep inside me, voicing that very familiar greeting, an Amharic term that I had never forgotten, a term that meant not only "hello," but also "may God give you health."

FURTHER READING

Daniel Coleman. *The Scent of Eucalyptus: A Missionary Childhood in Ethiopia*. New Brunswick: Goose Lane Editions, 2003.

Graham Hancock. *The Sign and the Seal: The Quest for the Lost Ark of the Covenant*. New York: Touchstone, 1993.

Ryszard Kapućiśki. *The Emperor: Downfall of an Autocrat*. New York: Vintage Books, 1989.

Barbara Kingsolver. *The Poisonwood Bible*. New York: Harper Perennial, 1999.

Margaret Meyers. *Swimming in the Congo*. Minneapolis: Milkweed Editions, 1995.

Nega Mezlekia. *Notes from the Hyena's Belly: Memories of My Ethiopian Boyhood*. Toronto: Penguin Books, 2000.

Elaine Neil Orr. *Gods of Noonday: A White Girl's African Life*. Charlottesville: University of Virginia Press, 2003.

ACKNOWLEDGMENTS

Memory is shaped by perception. I keep and store what matters to me personally. As a result, what may seem insignificant to others may be vital to me, and my story of the past cannot be the same story told by others, not even those closest to me.

Having said that, I am deeply indebted to my parents and my brothers, who have lived through these events firsthand and experienced them in their own ways. They have graciously accepted my version of the past, helping me to be more accurate about facts but also giving me the freedom to tell it as I remember it, even when that involved reflecting on them.

Memory does not operate like video footage, so I have had to re-create scenes and conversations based on the stills in my mind or the snippets of speech that could be recalled. Undoubtedly, I have also gotten some events out of sequence due to the distance between me and those early childhood memories. However, I have tried to remain faithful to the events as I remembered them or as I learned about them from others. I have been particularly helped by my mother's photo albums and by the remarkable series of letters that she preserved as an account of our life in Ethiopia.

In a few instances, names have been changed to protect identities. Also, I have taken the liberty in the chapter "And I'll Fly Away" to retell another child's experience as I imagined it, because I was not there to see it taking place.

There are many people who have helped to make this book a reality, and I must thank them. First and foremost, I thank my wife, who has believed in me even when I did not. She is a faithful and wise critic. I have been encouraged and challenged by a marvelous mentor, Patricia Foster, who keeps asking all the hardest and most vital questions. I am indebted to my editor, Anne Seiwerath, who skillfully showed the way toward more unity and completeness as I finished the book. I also want to recognize a number of insightful readers who have offered invaluable feedback and support: Judy, Andy, Amy, Tom, Sarah, Faith, Daniel, Drew, Tiare, and Allison. I could not have done it without you.

Bread Loaf and the Bakeless Prizes

The Katharine Bakeless Nason Literary Publication Prizes were established in 1995 to expand Bread Loaf Writers' Conference's commitment to the support of emerging writers. Endowed by the L. Z. Francis Foundation, the prizes commemorate Middlebury College patron Katharine Bakeless Nason and launch the publication career of a poet, fiction writer, and creative nonfiction writer annually. Winning manuscripts are chosen in an open national competition by a distinguished judge in each genre. Winners are published by Houghton Mifflin Company in a Mariner paperback original.

2005 JUDGES

Philip Levine, poetry
Francine Prose, fiction
Edward Hoagland, creative nonfiction